Tales of the Everingham Family

Gathered by Kevin Everingham

Containing family legends, newspaper articles,
Genealogical research, family folklore, myth
and news about the Everingham family.

The material printed here, is exactly
as it was originally written with phonetic
spelling and colorful wording of the era.

Published by the

Everingham
Family History
Archives

(C)2017

www.everingham.com/family

Story Index;

Page
COLONIAL EVERINGHAMS

7   Earliest Everingham in America and a revolt against the King's Governor, 1701.
8   Relatives Jailed for having debt!
9   The Everingham Sawmill, at Toms River, New Jersey

STORIES OF MURDER

10   *"Dead in Bed"* A bigamist killer in Ohio
11   A 1923 murder in Illinois
12   A father's vengeance
12   Young Roscoe Everingham killed in 1899
12   Murder of a Church Bishop in 1170

STORIES OF DRINKING

13   A 2 gallon jug *"twas a bad companion"*
13   Sadie Everingham jailed for a summer!
13-14 Ward Everingham of New York, found dying in the road in 1912.
14   John Everingham, Fayetteville, NY.
14-15 Prominent farmer dies while drunk
15   Horrific Sawmill accident of 1900!
15   Expensive drink in Ontario in 1917.
15   William Everingham, 1893
16   James Everingham, 1902
16   A humorous deaf drinker 1904
16   A beating in New Jersey
16   *Unknown* T.C. Everingham, beer thief
17   American book and movie about a A drunken *"Evringham"* character.

EVERINGHAM'S AT SEA

18   Everinghams at sea in 14th & 15th century
18   1834 Pirates discovered
18   1804 The Brig *Charleston* advertisement
19-20 1835 Trial of the Barnegat pirates
20   Pirate trial outcome.

Page
EVERINGHAM'S AT SEA

21   An actual shipwreck letter from 1852.
21-22 About Capt. Andrew Jackson Evernham
22   A shipping advertisement from 1803
22-25 Privateer schooner named *Saucy Jack*
23   1814 article about the *Saucy Jack*
24   Capture of the *Pellham*, privateer Captain Chazel's ship log entry.
25   Story about an unlucky privateer ship
25-26 Muntiny aboard the *General Armstrong*
26   Midshipman James Everingham from England, during the war of 1812.
27   A little about the sloop yacht *Petrel*
28   Rebecca Everingham postage stamp.
28   The aristocratic Wadley family
28-29 The *Rebecca Everingham* steamboat
29   A river horror burning of a southern riverboat steamer with loss of life.
29   1884 Steamboat horror article.

GUN ACCIDENTS

30   Louis Everingham shot with a 38.
30   Civil War hero loses his son to gun accident in Michigan, 1898.
31   Woman shot but saved by her corset. *Mrs. Joseph Everingham of NY.*
31   Hiram Lymburner killed hunting
31   Lethal gun cleaning accident 1881

Page
OTHER ACCIDENTS

32   6 year old tumbles over a moving train, in 1894 and lives!
32   Car accident 1922 and another in 1923.
32   Norman Everingham accident 1922.
32-33 Bob Everingham Jr. farm accident
33   New Jersey Mayor dies in accident 1960
33   Mayor Everingham's wife dies in crash
34   1893 Railroad secretary James Everingham dies at work.
45   Man killed by a trolley in 1917.
45   Man killed on train tracks 1892.

SHOCKING NEWS

4   Heroics of Paul Everingham
34-35 Joseph Everham, early American actor and co-star Octavia Allen.
35   A 19th century tabloid story.
36   A close call during the civil war, 1864
36   1891 sad asylum story about Civil war veteran Charles Everingham of NY.
36   1924 Addie Everham suicide.
37   An attempted robbery in NJ, 1917.
37   Charles Everham's marriage problems
38   Suicide of Cory Everingham in 1901.
38   Olive Everingham breaks both wrists.
39   Grocer's wife dies of blood poisoning.
39   M.C. Everingham store advertisement
40   The troubled daughters of Cyrus.
41   14 year old rescues his family.

OTHER FAMILY NEWS

41   Indian troubles 1919 in New York.
41-42 14 year old rescues his family, 2008
42   Henry doing the right thing in 1911.
43   John Everingham quits carriage business
43   American artist Millard Everingham
44   Inventive farmer in New York.
45   Man killed by a trolley in 1917.
45   Man killed on train tracks 1892.
      "Hiram Everingham Jr."
45   A Everingham family author
45   Harvard post for a Kansan 1909.

46   Red Baron's victim #39.
47   Everingham road in Nedrow, NY.
47-48 1889 family fight among in-laws.
48   Patrol car stolen in 1941.
48-49 Civil War Captain organizes reunion.
49-50 College dropout at Michigan becomes head of a major U.S. corporation
51   Gold rush fever in the family.
52   A family dog travels over 100 miles.
53   Everingham brothers in the newspaper business in New York.
54-55 The Everingham Millions!
56-57 A link to the Iroquois Nation
59-60 Bibliography

KNOCKS AWAY PISTOL AND BEATS ROBBERS.

PAUL EVERINGHAM

Paul Everingham, 14 Astor street, who last Wednesday evening put two holdup men to flight after giving them a beating, is a British veteran of the Boer war. He was at Division and Astor streets when attacked. One of the highwaymen pointed a revolver at him. Instead of complying with an order to hold up his hands Everingham pushed aside the weapon and knocked down both robbers, who got up and ran.

This surprising Newspaper article is about an unknown Paul Everingham, possibly a recent immigrant to America. This photo is unverified but shows his British uniform from the 2nd Boer War which ended in 1902.

The earliest known Everingham in America takes part in a colonial revolt!

Jeremiah Everingham was likely an English immigrant and possible father of five or six of the first Everinghams known to have lived in the American colonies. He was likely born between 1670 and 1680. It is known that he was present in New Jersey in 1701 according to court session minutes of Middletown, New Jersey. Previous genealogy records have stated that the first Everingham in America came in 1703, but a hand written court record proved that is probably incorrect. — — — —

In 1701 there was an ongoing dispute between supporters of Andrew Hamilton and supporters of Jeremiah Basse, each claimed to be the rightful Governor of the province of New Jersey. After New York and New Jersey had been taken by the Dutch, a peace treaty had been signed and the land was given back to the control of England. Since ownership deeds may have been destroyed, or simply reassigned by England, they claimed ownership of a large strip of land including; Middleton, Shrewsbury & much of Monmouth county, in the middle of New Jersey.

Land lost by the people of New Jersey and tax issues brought growing unrest. Many were now against the new Governor Hamilton. Tax riots and land issues were campaign stands of Governor Basse, who had been replaced as New Jersey Governor by England's King in 1699.

In the court session minutes of Middletown, New Jersey, March 25, 1701, it is known that a riotous uprising took place involving a man named Jeremiah Everingham.

Court opened that day focused on Moses Butterworth who was accused of piracy. Butterworth had confessed that he had sailed with Captain William Kidd in the East Indies. As examinations began, A man named Samuel Willett started an uproar when he stated that the Governor and Justices present had no authority to hold court. Willett had control of several men with guns and organized a drummer to make noise disrupting the proceedings. Thirty to forty men came into court, some with arms and some with clubs. In a scuffle with the court officials, Richard and Benjamin Borden were wounded.

The official **1701** record stated this:

*The people including; Safety Grover, Richard Borden, Benjamin Borden, Obadiah Holmes, Obadiah Bowne, Nicholas Stevens, George Cook, Benjamin Cook, Richard Osborne, Samuel Willett, Garret Wall, James Bollen, Samuel Foreman, William Hunter, Jonathan Stout, James Stout, William Hendricks, John Bray, William Smith, Gershom Mott, Abner Hough, George Allen, John Cox, John Vaughn, Elisha Lawrence, Zebulon Clayton, James Grover jr, Richard Davis, **Jeremiah Everingham**, Joseph Ashton with others to the number of about one hundred persons did traitorously seize the Governor and the Justices, the Kings Attorney-General and Secretary and the Clerk of the Court, and the Under-Sheriff and kept them under guard as prisoners from Tuesday the twenty-fifth of March till the Saturday following being the twenty-ninth of the same month and then released them.*

(Gavin Drummond, clerk.)

It is most likely that **Jeremiah Everingham** would not have been named by the court clerk if he was not an adult involved in this incident. If we ask ourselves why Jeremiah would risk such an act, it is easy to imagine that he was either a supporter of Governor Basse, or had lost land or property. It is also highly unlikely that Jeremiah would have risked his livelihood unless he was an impassioned adult that was fighting for lost property or rights. The only other feasible possibility is that he was involved with, or a supporter of someone on trial that day. Jeremiah Everingham must have been born in the mid to later 1600's and probably prior to 1680. (*since this incident took place in 1701*) This means that he is the oldest generation of known Everinghams documented in the American colonies, to my knowledge.

Nothing else has been found to give us more insight into this event but upon release of the court officials, those men named by the clerk would have likely been placed on wanted lists. It is likely that Jeremiah would have went into hiding if he had not been arrested. Involvement in an event like this could have lead to jail time, property seizure or even a death sentence. It is unlikely that some type of attempted prosecution could have been avoided. At this time, there have been no other records of Jeremiah, only harsh possibilities of what may have happened.

Early Colonial American relatives were jailed for debt!

Imagine being put in jail for having debt that you can't pay and then having everything you own taken away to cover that debt. And if you still had debt, *you just stay in jail*! It happened prior to the 19th century in America and Europe. Sometimes the amount of debt was quite small. It's hard to imagine since our society in the 21st century is based on borrowing money that you don't have and the concept of credit. In Colonial America, men were arrested for having debt and then unable to make money to pay the debt since they were in jail, their property was auctioned off to cover the debt.

Actual Colonial records show that this happened to our ancestors. Monmouth county, New Jersey; *By order of the Honorable John Anderson, John Taylor and John Wardell, James Lawrence Esquires, four of the Judges of the Court of Common Pleas for the said County, that **James Everingham**, Prisoner for debt, in said jail, was this twenty-first day of March, **1770**, qualified to the Schedule of his estate, pursuant to the late Act of Assembly, An Act for the relief of insolvent debtors, made this present tenth year of his Majesty's reign. Now this is to give notice to the creditors of said debtor, that they be together at the Court House of said County, on the 25th day of April next, to show cause, if they have, why the said debtor's Estate should not be assigned for the use of his creditors, and his body discharged from his confinement pursuant to said Act. ~ Monmouth jail, March 21, 1770 .*

A similar notice exists for a **Thomas Everingham** which was dated January **1771**. It is probable that James and Thomas were brothers or relatives. These legal notices were setting up the sale of, or forfeiture of their land and property to pay debts owed. Meanwhile, the men were kept in jail, not because they had committed crimes but because they owed money that was not yet paid. While in jail, they were of course unable to make money that they needed to pay the debts.

Family genealogists will recognize the related spouse names of *Gibertson* and *Robins,* in the record that follows; *(from the colonial court of common pleas records of 1771)* "*The Judges of the court of common pleas for said county of Monmouth,... Thomas Stricklan, John Vanderippe, Mathew Woolfe, Abraham Myer, Herman Gibertson, James Everingham, Daniel Robins, Charles Williams and Ann Jones, <u>prisoners for debt</u> in the jail of said county, having been duly sworn and filed their schedules, pursuant to the late act of assembly of said province, entitled, An Act for the relief of insolvent debtors, made in the tenth year of his Majesty's reign, and in the year of our lord **1769**.*" They posted that information in local newspapers to give notice to the creditors of the debtors listed, that they be together at the court house in Monmouth, New Jersey, on the sixteenth day of December *Annoque Domini* 1771, to show cause before the said judges, if any they have, why the said prisoners should not be discharged from their confinement, pursuant to the said act. In other words, the creditors were being asked to show up and explain if additional debt was owed to keep these people in jail longer, or give reason why they should not be released.

By modern standards, there is no doubt that England's **eighteenth century laws were unjust regarding the lower classes.** Under old English law, a person could be arrested as an insolvent debtor for an unpaid obligation of only a few shillings.

Although the colonists, under England's tight control, were unable to make major changes to the laws, they did eventually manage to make reforms in some of England's legal procedures. One of those reforms pertained to insolvent debtors like those listed here. It does not take a great deal of legal knowledge to realize if the person was confined in jail, he or she could not earn money to pay their creditors. Corrupt creditors could find ways to get men jailed long enough, to see their property and lands auctioned off or given to the creditor. At times the highest bidder could be the creditor who had them jailed to begin with! A very corruptible system by any standard of measurement.

An Act Abolishing imprisonment for Debt, was not approved until February 19, 1830. It constituted the first major change to the colonial insolvent debtor laws. Henceforth, no person could be confined in jail for debt, except in cases of fraud.

The Everingham Sawmill, at Toms River, New Jersey

According to a 422 page history book called, "*A History of Monmouth and Ocean Counties*" by Edwin Salter, published in 1890, there was once a sawmill known as the *Everingham sawmill*. A section of the book lists grist mills and saw mills first erected in modern-day Ocean County, New Jersey. It reports the Everingham sawmill was built on the north branch of Toms River in **1750** in Monmouth county, New Jersey. The earliest industry in the area at that time was lumber, coal and boat building.

It is known that a Thomas Everingham and a Henry Everingham were among tax payers in Upper Freehold N.J. in 1731. Henry Everingham listed in tax records is probably the same Henry who died in 1752. By 1758 a William and a Joseph Everingham were paying taxes there. This area was part of Monmouth County and was later separated and named Ocean County, New Jersey in 1850.

No document has been found yet to show who built the Everingham sawmill, but it is probable that Joseph, Thomas, William or Henry could have been owners. These men are possible sons or grandsons of Jeremiah Everingham discussed on page seven. Of those four men, Henry, Joseph or Thomas were all possible suspects to have been the man responsible for building or operating the mill.

According to family memoirs written by Florence Nelson Mintle, Henry Evernham was an owner of the sawmill. In her notes and among other family researchers, it is said that the Everingham sawmill was destroyed by the British during the Revolutionary war. There are many stories of the British burning homes and specifically mills during that era. In 1782 there was an attack on Toms River area that left the town in burned ruins. There is no proof that I've found, detailing the Everingham Mill being burned, and Mrs. Mintle doesn't know if Henry Everingham inherited it or purchased it. This is interesting information since the Henry Evernham that she identifies as the owner, was born in the 1760's and was a child when the Revolutionary war

started. He may be connected in some way and I believe that the Henry whom Mrs. Mintle identifies, was a *Smith & Wheelwright* by occupation. That information comes from another book; *Fare to Midlands*, by Henry Charleton Beck.

There was another, older Henry Everingham in the same area who married Rachel Robins. That Henry was dead by 1752. From the "*NationStudy*" web site, it is known that; Rachel (Robins) and her husband Henry Everingham had 80 acres that they bought from Jacob Robins in **1727**. Was this the land that the Everingham Mill would later be built on? Was it in the right general area of New Jersey? If they had built it just 2 years before Henry's death, maybe his sons operated it. Henry and Rachel had at least five or six sons.

Much of the early Everingham family history in America can be traced to these five counties in New Jersey.

9

Murder;

This chapter will discuss Everingham's and their relatives who were involved in murder cases. Murder is always a headline grabbing news item and some of the cases involving the Everingham family or people close to them is no different. We will start with the case of "**Dead in Bed**" as the headline reads. This murder happened in Cleveland, Ohio, May 11, 1896.

Royce James Everingham from New York had married his first wife Lottie Case, in 1893. According to their marriage record, they married at Cuyahoga county, Ohio. The marriage was short lived and by 1895, Lottie had been charged with bigamy; *being married to two men.* On September 11, 1895, A newspaper headline from Maysville, Kentucky, read; **Guilty of Bigamy** in Ashland, Ohio. According to the article, Lottie Case of Cleveland plead guilty to bigamy and was sentenced to one year in the penitentiary. At that time, her husbands were; Royce J. Everingham of Cleveland, Ohio, and John Hyman of Savannah, Georgia. The murder story likely connects to Lottie, but since her name is never given, it is not absolute.

Read the story below *(& right)* and

DEAD IN BED.

A Female Convict Recently Pardoned, Under Arrest Under Suspicion of Murder.

CLEVELAND, O., May 11.—Alex. McKenzie, a clerk in the offices of the Pennsylvania railroad, was found dead in bed Sunday afternoon, and Mrs. Jas. Everingham, the woman with whom he was living, was drunk and in the same bed. The man had died from a dose of sulphate of zinc, which the woman had given him. She was placed under arrest, charged with murder. The woman was pardoned from the penitentiary four, weeks ago. She was serving a term for bigamy. She came here four weeks ago and was living with McKenzie, leading the neighbors to suppose they were man and wife. The reason for the crime is thought to be an insurance policy made in her favor.

decide if it's the same lady or not. About 8 months later,... On May 11, 1896 the Scranton Pennsylvania Tribune and several Ohio newspapers reported that Alexander McKenzie, a clerk for the Pennsylvania railroad, had been poisoned by zinc. He was found dead in bed, and Mrs. James Everingham, the woman McKenzie was living with, was found drunk beside him. Mr. McKenzie had died from a dose of sulphate of zinc which the woman had given him. She was placed under arrest and charged with murder. The woman had been pardoned from the penitentiary weeks earlier for a bigamy charge. She had been living with McKenzie for about a month. I have never found follow-up stories to this article but at the time of the event, the police believed she did it for insurance money.

Mr. Everingham went on to marry at least 3 more times in Ohio. It's easy to make the assumption that he may have had trust issues after starting out married life with Lottie.

Guilty of Bigamy.

ASHLAND, O., Sept. 11.—Lottie Case of Cleveland pleaded guilty to bigamy, and was sentenced to one year in the penitentiary. Her husbands were Royce J. Everingham of Cleveland, and John Hyman of Savannah.

1923 Murder in Illinois

The article shown here is a little hard to read, but the headline reads; "**Shipment of body delayed pending an investigation, make two arrests**" Police were seeking a man and woman in connection with a mysterious case. They believed the victim was clubbed over the head and robbed by the couple and possibly by the employees where Mr. Everingham was eating. Two men were arrested and Sheriff Timm of Vermillion county Illinois was seeking another man and a woman in connection with the mysterious death of **Harry G. Everingham**. Harry was found dead Monday night in an all-night lunch wagon in downtown Danville. Police were told that Everingham dropped dead after eating a lunch and death was attributed to heart troubles. The Sheriff was later informed that Everingham had several hundred dollars, which were missing from the body.

Preparations had been made to send the body to relatives in Erie, Pennsylvania but this was delayed to allow an autopsy. The autopsy disclosed the cause of death was a hemorrhage of the brain due to a heavy blow to the head.

James Mittman, night cook on the lunch wagon and Harry Dillinger were arrested and a search was begun for the man and woman who are known to have been sitting at the counter when Everingham died. Authorities express belief that Everingham was hit on the head after he displayed his money in paying for his lunch. They believe that the money was divided up by the assailants.

Harry G. Everingham was born in Warsaw, Wyoming county, New York, about 1874. As a young man in the 1890's he went by the stage name of "**Harry Anden**" and worked as a contortionist in Troy, New York. Harry married Mable Bond, a song and dance lady who worked at the same place. A newspaper article in 1895 says *"They are both first class artists. Everingham is the son of John W. Everingham and is making a success of his chosen profession."* At some point, the marriage to Mable was dissolved. Harry left his home-town village years ago and enlisted in Company A, of the 1st Cavalry. He served in the Spanish War. Another newspaper article dated July 11, 1918 reported about Harry's military service - *"Harry G. Everingham, a son of John W. Everingham and a former Warsaw boy is in the balloon section of the army and is now stationed at Richmond, Virginia. He is in the Balloon General Supply Depot, U.S. Army. He expects to make a couple of trips to France this fall. Mr. Everingham enlisted last April for the Balloon squadron."*

Harry's father died in 1922 at the Wyoming county farm. His mother has been dead for several years. A sister resided in Cleveland and he had four uncles, Thomas Everingham of Batavia, Joseph Everingham, Silver Springs, Charles Everingham, Castile, and Frank Everingham of LeRoy, N.Y. The Louis Everingham listed in the article was actually his brother.

SHIPMENT OF BODY DELAYED PENDING AN INVESTIGATION, MAKE TWO ARRESTS

Seek Man and Woman, Too, In Connection With Mysterious Case

THINK VICTIM CLUBBED AFTER DISPLAYING MONEY

(By Special Wire to The Courier.)
Danville, Ill., Jan. 31.—Two men are under arrest and Sheriff Timm of Vermillion county tonight is seeking another man and woman in connection with the mysterious death here of Harry G. Everingham, formerly of Warsaw, N. Y., found dead Monday night in an all-night lunch wagon in downtown Danville.

Police were told Everingham dropped dead after eating a lunch and death was attributed to heart trouble, but Sheriff Timm later was informed that Everingham had several hundred dollars, none of which was found after his death.

Delay Shipment to Erie.

Preparations had been made to send the body to relatives in Erie, Pa., today, but this was delayed to allow an autopsy, which disclosed the cause of death was a hemorrhage of the brain due to a heavy blow on [the head.]

James Mittman, night cook on the lunch wagon, and Harry Dillinger were arrested and search was begun for the man and woman, who are known to have been sitting at the counter when Everingham died.

Authorities express belief that Everingham was hit on the head after he displayed his money in paying for his lunch, and that the money was divided by his assailants.

Harry C. Everingham was born in Warsaw about forty-nine years ago. He left the village years ago, enlisting and serving in the Spanish War. His father died a few years ago at the Wyoming county farm. His mother has been dead several years. A sister resides in Cleveland and he has four uncles, Thomas Everingham of Batavia, Joseph Everingham, Silver Springs, Charles Everingham, Castile, and Louis, Erie, Pa.

When in Warsaw he followed no particular line of work, but did odd jobs. After he left Warsaw very little was known of him.

Thanks to fellow family genealogist Kimball Everingham for sharing his research of the first part of this story;

A Father's Vengeance

Headline from the Teutopolis Press, **1898**. June 22, Driven to desperation by wrongs that can not properly be named in respectable society.

Herbert G. Everingham yesterday afternoon shot and mortally wounded Samuel L. Lindsay, his brother-in-law. The shooting occurred about 4:40 p.m. and Lindsay's death at the City Hospital nearly five hours later.

The provocation for this homicide can only be alluded to here. Suffice it to say that Everingham's little 13-year old daughter, Bessie, confessed to her mother yesterday morning that her "*Uncle Sam*" had, eleven months ago, done her a most cruel wrong and that their relations culminated a week ago in the administration of medicine that came near to causing the child's death.

This story was also told in a New York newspaper called the Sea Cliff News, Saturday, July 2, 1898;

Samuel L. Lindsey, a bookkeeper, was shot and killed in St. Louis, Missouri, by his brother-in-law, Herbert G. Everingham. The latter's little daughter had confessed to her mother that Lindsey had assaulted her and the father took summary vengeance.

Young man killed in Illinois, 1899

In 1899 a Murder took place in Illinois. Lee Roscoe Everingham was born in the 1880's in Hutsonville, Crawford county, Illinois. He went by the name Roscoe. Very little is known about his life since he died fairly young. He was the son of Nelson and Ida (Salsbury) Everingham.

Argus, Robinson, IL Oct. 1899

"Roscoe Everingham was found dead in a buggy, having been shot." October 15, 1899

Murder of a Church Bishop

The last murder story reaches back generations into the history of the Everingham homeland; England. When researching the early Everingham's, it would be impossible to overlook one of the most influential families, the Everingham's of Laxton. Laxton was a great estate containing a castle, rectory and many important buildings and land holdings. One estate called Kirkburn, was part of the family holdings and was the base of a fair was held each year to celebrate "*Thomas the Martyr*". Records show that royalty and even Kings stayed at Laxton when the Everingham Knights and Lords controlled it. Since the fair was an Everingham family celebration, I decided to investigate who Thomas the martyr was. Learning about Thomas is sure to lead to stories of murder since he was called a martyr!

The Fair at Laxton Castle no doubt celebrated the life and death of, Archbishop of Canterbury Thomas Becket. His story can be found in Chaucer's Canterbury Tales, and in other writings.

Thomas opposed King Henry II's Royal laws over church figures or over any *Law of God*. The church was very powerful at this time in history and this proved to be a thorn in King Henry's side. The King wanted to be the final say in law. King Henry and Thomas Becket were actually long-time friends but the King was not able to control as much as he wished because of Becket's beliefs. Becket and the King fought verbally many times over this issue, which ended in the year 1170. Four Knights made Thomas Becket a martyr when they killed him at Canterbury Cathedral, after most likely taking their orders from the King.

King Henry showed remorse over the loss of his *former* friend and allowed himself to be publically flogged by the Monks. Striking a King was punishable by death, so this was a grand gesture that Henry made to try to get back in the favor of the Church. The King also asked the Pope for forgiveness.

Thomas was later canonized a Saint, and the Cathedral became a place of religious pilgrimage.

In the 14th and 15th centuries when the Everingham family owned Laxton and chartered fairs with a celebration theme of *Thomas the Martyr*, these fairs were religious in nature and would likely have drawn people from all around as well as generated money.

Drinkers;

A group of the population abuses alcohol or have abused alcohol. This is a fact that has been present in almost all known recorded history of humans. Research has suggested that some vulnerability towards developing alcohol-related issues comes from genetics. Animal research has indicated that inheritance of alcohol or drug addictions can take many forms. Studies have demonstrated that various individual genes or groups of genes can shape very distinct responses to alcohol. How an individual processes alcohol may have a lot to do with proteins and enzymes present in their body. It may sound sexist but it is a biological fact that women generally do not process alcohol as efficiently as men. Although I do not believe there is definitive proof for alcoholism genetically in the Everingham family, the following stories take a quick look at some males and females who were caught overindulging in alcohol.

The first story comes from The Express, a Syracuse, New York Newspaper, dated Thursday, February 18, 1892.

'TWAS A BAD COMPANION,
A Two-Gallon Jug of Whiskey Misled Mr. Everingham

Charles Everingham of Jamesville drove to town Friday in a bob-sleigh and bought a two-gallon jug of whiskey. Later in the day he attracted considerable attention. He had drunk often from the jug and was on his knees in the sleigh, his arms and head hanging helplessly over the dash board. When near St. Paul's cathedral he fell out of the sleigh, but managed to crawl back again and occupied the same position. The team stopped, as if by instinct in front of the Station House, and Everingham was locked up, while the team was sent to the Candeo House barn. Saturday Everingham was reprimanded for intoxication and was discharged.

Another story (*shown top right*) tells of someone named **Sadie Everingham** who was sentenced to three months in jail for being drunk and disorderly! The article doesn't tell much about the case or if

Red Bank N.J. Register Newspaper, Wednesday, June 7, 1905

Will Spend the Summer in Jail.

Benjamin Tulliver, colored, and Sadie Everingham, white, both of Long Branch, were arrested last Wednesday for being drunk and disorderly. They were sent to the county jail for three months.

she was disorderly with Mr. Tulliver who was also named, but the details would be interesting considering they were sentenced to quite a lengthy jail stay for being disorderly. It is curious that they noted in the newspaper that he was a "*colored*" man and she was "*white*." Any conclusions drawn from this brief news would be mere guesses but there is much more to this story!

According to the Daily Sentinel, Thursday, April 13, 1911, **Ward Everingham** was arrested in Rome, New York. Ward was noted as a stranger in town, and was arraigned in city court that morning, charged with public intoxication. Ward had a bruised eye that looked as if it had come in contact with the sidewalk. He told the court that he wanted to get to Oneida and get to work. His sentence was suspended and he was released.

A man named **Ward Everingham** from Onondaga County, New York, was born about 1851. He may have been this same person. He had a brother who died at about age 14 and another brother who died young in 1862 during the Civil War. A third brother was a very successful farmer and inventor. About a year after this first event, Ward was found dying in the road, possibly from another drinking binge. A Syracuse New York Newspaper reported it; The Syracuse Herald,

Tuesday, March 12, 1912 , **FOUND DYING IN ROAD,** Everingham expires in hospital - Probably result of exposure, physicians say. Ward Everingham, 57 years old, who for the last seven years has been an inmate of the county home, was found lying unconscious in south Salina street about one-half mile south of Onondaga Valley shortly after 6 o'clock this morning by John Bailey, a milkman.

Everingham was removed to St. Joseph's hospital, where he died at 9 o'clock this morning. The case has been reported to Coroner George R. Kinne, who will make an investigation and have an autopsy performed on the body. There were no marks on the body which would show that death was the result of foul play. There is a possibility that the man sank exhausted on the road and that death came as the result of several hours exposure. Everingham had relatives living near Rockwell Springs, and up to about ten years ago, he made his home there. In 1905 he was taken into the County home. From that time on he has been an inmate at the institution off and on. Last Saturday he told one of the officers at the home that he was going to leave. He left in the afternoon and had not been seen by the authorities since.

This morning shortly after 6 o'clock John Bailey, a milkman owning a farm near the Indian reservation, was coming into the city by way of south Salina street to deliver milk. When he was about one-half mile south of Seneca street, Onondaga Valley, he saw a man lying in the road. He pulled up his horse just in time to stop the animal from trampling on the body. Bailey got out and he recognized the man as Everingham. Bailey took the man in his arms and placed him in the wagon. He then drove with all speed possible to the offices of Dr. S. Ellis Crane of Onondaga Valley. The physician ordered his immediate removal to a hospital. St. Joseph's ambulance was summoned and Everingham was taken to that institution.
He never regained consciousness.

Fayetteville N.Y. Weekly Recorder
Manlius Legal & Business Section,
Thursday, July 16, 1891
"John Everingham occupied the cooler Sunday and was fined three dollars for drunkeness the next morning."

The little bit of information about a Mr. John Everingham (*bottom left corner*) fined in 1891 is very hard to pinpoint.   In mid-New York State, there were actually several men named John Everingham. This John Everingham spent a night in jail and was fined three dollars. I don't find other stories of any John Everinghams being drunk, so it is likely that this was an isolated incident for this man. He lived quite close to Ward Everingham from the previous story and was probably a relative.

Man dies while drunk?

A lengthy story was printed in the Omaha Daily Bee, a Newspaper in Nebraska. It happened Saturday, Sept. 23, 1904.   The headline read; **"Dead in room and gas turned on, Prominent Farmer of Mills County the victim."** Furman H. Everingham, an old settler of Mills county and well known resident of Glenwood, was found dead in his room at Ogden hotel early yesterday morning, death having resulted from asphyxiation. The door and window were tightly closed and the room was filled with gas from a wide-open burner. It was after midnight Thursday that Everingham, who had frequently been a guest of the hotel before, appeared at the Ogden house and asked for a room. His manner, it is said, indicated that he had been drinking and his signature on the register was a mere scrawl. The night-clerk accompanied him to his room and before leaving him inquired if he understood how to turn off the gas. Everingham was somewhat indignant at the question being put to him and replied *of course I know how to turn off the light. I ain't no Rube, am I?* The window and transom over the door were both open, so the clerk states, when he left Everingham.

Everingham was 57 years of age and is survived by his wife and two children, a son and a daughter, the latter being married. Two weeks ago Everingham's house in Glenwood was struck by lightning and burned, he himself having a narrow escape from being burned. The wife at the time of the fire and since has been visiting relatives in New Jersey. Everingham's visit to Council Bluffs was to close a trade with John L. Price for a large farm in Nebraska, he having arranged to meet Mr. Price yesterday morning at 9 o'clock. Deceased dealt extensively in farm lands and owned a number of fine farms in Mills county, besides a number of houses and lots in Glenwood. Henry Everingham, proprietor of the commercial house in Glenwood, a brother of the dead man, came to the city on learning of his brother's tragic end, and took the body back to Glenwood, where the funeral will be held.

Spelling in several old records show that Furman spelled his last name Evernham. This is probably also how the family pronounced it. He was the son of Henry Evernham & Euphema Bucher. Henry had died in 1903. The family was previously from New Jersey.

Horrific Sawmill Accident

A headline in the Watertown Daily Times, N.Y. Saturday, June 2, 1900 tells of a horrific accident. - "*Philip Evingham, while intoxicated, fell upon a slab in a saw-mill at Belmont, NY, Friday, and his body was cut in two*." More is told about this situation since the story was so horrible, it naturally made it into several newspapers.

The Bolivar Breeze Newspaper, Thursday, June 7, 1900 told more details. "**HORRIBLE ACCIDENT NEAR BELMONT** --- Philip Evingham, aged 39, fell across a buzz-saw and his body was cut in two, thursday afternoon.

Philip Evingham, 39 years of age was instantly killed by falling upon a cut-off saw in M.E. Horner's portable saw-mill on the Bower timber lot, about two miles south of Belmont, says the Belmont dispatch. The accident occurred about half past five o'clock Thursday afternoon. Mr. Ervingham has been about the mill all the afternoon, but had not been working there. His regular occupation had been that of a woodsman on the job, but the day before he had been loading lumber at Scio for Mr. Horner and on Thursday he was laying off. Near the two foot cut-off saw at which George Dickinson was working was a pile of slippery slabs. While Evingham was crossing these he slipped and thrust out his right hand. It hit the saw and his fingers were thrown in several directions. He kept on slipping, and turning around, his other arm came in contact with the saw and was cut off, and his body then fell directly upon the buzzing steel, which entered below the stomach and cut to the spinal column. It killed him instantly, and he made no conscious outcry. John Roberts, Albert Sortore, Isaac Pendleton, R. Cook and Lew Hildrath were in the mill at the time. George Dickinson who was at the saw, fell in dead faint as he realized that he couldn't save Evingham and the horror of the accident came over him.

George Horner and Clyde Austin took the body to Belmont in a platform wagon, and then to the home of the victim's brother, John Evingham, on the Rogers farm. The wife of Philip Everingham died several years ago, but he has five children under 15 years surviving. They have resided with relatives for some time.

The Daily Colonist, Victoria, B.C.
Tuesday, January 2, 1917

Expensive Drink

Niagara Falls, Ontario, January 1, Frank Everingham, this city was fined two hundred dollars, the lowest fine, or three months in jail for giving Henry Parks, a friend, a drink from a flask of liquor.

Constable Bough saw him do it. Everingham decided that he could earn the two hundred in jail easier, and went to Welland. Parks was fined fifteen dollars for being drunk, as it was his second offense.

Syracuse New York Journal Daily
October 16, 1893

"William Everingham of Onondaga is listed among others who were charged with intoxication but were allowed to go."

The Evening Hearld, Syracuse, NY, October, 1902

DRINKING, FIGHTING, AND THE PENALTY FOR LYING

Charles Cowell, Fred Plaisted and James Everingham were arrested in an East Water street saloon last night and locked up on the charge of public intoxication. Everingham claimed that the other men stole his watch.

Everingham was allowed to go in Police court this morning. Plaisted was given six months and Cowell was held as he lied to the Justice. He said that he lived in Midland avenue and gave a number not to be found in the directory. He also said that he worked in a sash and blind factory. A investigation showed that he did not work there. He will go to the penitentiary.

The Evening Hearld, Syracuse, NY, January 11, 1904

"Pretty Well, Thank You."
James Everingham gave this answer when he was asked his age in court.

James Everingham of Center street is all but deaf. He was arraigned in police court today for public intoxication.

"*How old are you?*" asked the clerk.

"*Oh, I'm pretty well, thank you.*" he answered.

Another question was given him.

"*Ask my wife, she's right back here,*" he said.

He was asked if he had been drunk.

"*I might have been,*" he answered.

He was released.

RED BANK REGISTER.

VOLUME XXII. NO. 49   RED BANK, N.J., WEDNESDAY, MAY 30, 1900.   PAGES 9 TO 16.

Helped Others Beat His Wife.

Mrs. Craig Wells of Long Branch went to Mrs. Sarah Everingham's house at that place last week in search of her husband. She found her husband sitting alongside of Mrs. Everingham. Mrs. Everingham's son, Howard, was also in the room, and Mrs. Wells says that the three attacked her and beat her until she was black and blue. Mr. Wells and Mrs. Everingham and her son were arrested and in default of bail they were sent to Freehold to await the action of the grand jury.

I have no idea who is involved in the beating listed above in the Red Bank Register Newspaper.

I never found follow-up information about what happened to these people in this strange incident.

Below is news from the North Platte Semi-Weekly Tribune, N. Platte, Nebraska, Tuesday, August 6, 1895. I found nothing else about this article and have no idea who it was.

The outcome of the Lodge Pole beer stealing case is as follows, according the Express: T. C. Everingham and I. H. Barrett have been discharged from the employ of the Union Pacific for alleged complicity in the beer case, and night operator Cowdin has been notified that he must pay for the beer because it was taken while he was on duty.

American Book and Movie with "Evringham" characters.

Jewel is a black & white 50 minute movie by universal films, made in the U.S. in 1915. This was the era of silent films and was based on a novel published in 1903 by Clara Louise Burnham. Clara wrote 26 novels between 1881 and 1925. Her books often tackled the subject of Christian Science and have sold half a million copies.

The story of Jewel takes place in the fictional home of the wealthy and dysfunctional Evringham family, headed by a bitter paternal figure who is disappointed in his sons, one deceased and the other a recovering alcoholic. The story focuses on a little girl named Julia Evringham, who is called Jewel by her mother. The story also focuses on Jewel's religious beliefs and how she uses them to deal with her life situations. The story is continued in a sequel book called "Jewel's Story Book."

The original movie starred: Ella Hall (as Jewel "*see poster left*"), Rupert Julian (as Mr. Evringham), Frank Elliot (as Lawrence Evringham), Hylda Hollis (Mrs. Lawrence Evringham), Brownie Brownell (as Eliose), T.D. Crittenden, (as Harry Evringham), Dixie Carr (as Julia), Gibson Gowland (as Dr. Ballard)

The film was remade in 1923, into a 84 minute movie and called "*A Chapter in Her Life*".

Everinghams at Sea;

Over hundreds of years, many Everinghams have been involved in the shipping trade as dock workers, merchants, captains and even pirates or privateers. One of the oldest references that I've found comes from notes during the reign of King Edward III (1327-1377). Early prestigious Everinghams of England were known to have links to this King. A commission was composed of **Thomas Everingham** and James Knighley, who were supposed to arrest ships in Hull. Everingham had acted as a justice of jail delivery, and a collector of loans for the expedition to Gascony.

Much later, during the reign of King Richard III (1483-1485). The King was tending to matters of civil unrest in his lands. A French Fleet attacked which resulted in the loss of English ships. One ship and it's Captain, **Sir Thomas Everingham** was lost near the shore of the castle *Scarborough* in **1484**. Scarborough was an important port for the wool trade, and was attacked several times by enemy forces. King Richard III was the last monarch to enter the grounds at Scarborough. He resided at the castle in 1484 while forming a fleet to fight the Tudors, a struggle he lost along with his life the following year in 1485.

PIRATES!

1834 New York Courier & Enquirer
THE BANDITTI DISCOVERED

About two months since the schooner *James Fisher* bound hence for Philadelphia and ladened with a cargo valued at $8,000, was in a gale of wind cast on the beach at Barnegat inlet, Monmouth county, New Jersey. The night after she went ashore she was boarded by a gang of about 100 land pirates, who carried off the whole of her cargo in small boats. Three weeks after the wreck of the *James Fisher*, the schooner *Henry Franklin*, with a full cargo, bound from Boston to Philadelphia was, under similar adverse circumstances, stranded at the same place. A band of pirates numbering more than 100 with faces blackened,

and otherwise disguised, made a descent on the stranded vessel, ordered the mate and seamen to leave and threatened death. A mate and crew armed themselves and returned to the wreck but in the interim, the plunderers had fled. Later an agent of the insurance company discovered and arrested one of the most prominent leaders of the gang, a Captain Hulsehart. He had sought out and secured the sailors in plundering the *Henry Franklin*, one of them called himself **Holcomb Everingham**, but others refused to give names. The prisoners were lodged in Newark jail in New Jersey. Another leader of the pirates Capt. Edward Wainwright was arrested. And Isaac, Abraham and John, sons of John Allen Sr. were arrested. Tavern-keeper Reuben Grant, and store keeper Joseph Bunnell, farmer Thomas Bunnell, and Zepthaniah Johnson were arrested. The investigator states that nearly two thirds of the inhabitants of the district of four or five miles are implicated. Farmers, storekeepers, sailors and heads of families have absconded and left their property from the retribution which awaits them.

Over 100 people were gathered-up, which led to a big trial for Piracy in Trenton, NJ 1835.

Trial of the Barnegat Pirates

(*it should be noted that the only "Holcomb" that I am aware of would be* **George Holcomb Everingham** *born 1819 New Jersey. He would have been about 15 years old at the time of this incident. His mother was later widowed and married Jesse Platt. So Holcomb had "Platt" step-siblings. He also had connections to the Grant, Cornelius and Britton families.*)
This is a transcript of a trial and is a little hard to follow;

Jeptha Johnson, (*one of the gang turned state's evidence*) testified that he lived on Squire Platt's place, and went in company with Job Platt, Stacy Stockton, Joseph Britton, and B. Lewis to Herring's about 12 o'clock at night, when they all took something to drink. There were a great many person there. In the after part of the night, went to the wreck with others. Prisoner said to witness and others, it was best to get his coffee and fish and go on board his vessel. Witness was not consulted with, to go down for the purpose of plundering. Not long after this, he was asked by Captain Wainwright, if he could pull a strong oar. Wainwright and Squire Platt went with witness down to the vessel. About thirty men were there. Saw prisoner, Job Platt, Joel Platt, Isaac Allen, Abraham Allen, and William Brindley on board, not doing much of anything. Did not see what they were doing. Saw William Brindley take a bag off; witness took a bag of coffee, and cut off with it toward the inlet. Saw Joseph Matthews roll a barrel of mackerel and a box of soap was burst open on the sand. Knew nothing about the division of the spoils.

Cross-examined—Squire Platt asked if they had not a mind to go down to the vessel - nothing was said about going to plunder. No talk on the way to the beach. Joseph Britton, Amos Grant, John Potter and John Bennett inquired for coffee afterward, but got none.

Thursday, Oct. 8

The first witness examined this morning was **Holcomb Everingham**, a boy of fifteen or sixteen years old, (*prior cook of Capt. Hulsehart aboard the New-Jersey, and subpoenaed as witness for the government*) lives between Cedar creek and John river, on the beach. Went with the prisoner, Cornelius, Joel Platt, and Hamilton Allen, to the tent near the wreck, toward dusk; then went back to Herring's, afterward returned to the tent with others he met on the way, and sat by the fire a short time.

Went to Herring's again; stayed awhile, when the prisoner sent him on board for some candles.

Young Herring went with him, and assisted in bringing the yawl ashore; brought it to a point of the beach, inside; prisoner told him to do so. After he had been there some time, desired him to bring her opposite Herring's house. Brought her there. James Stewart was with him. After which, the prisoner said he must take her to the point of the beach, with captain E. Wainwright's boat, Ephriam Atterson's yawl, and Herring's skiff. Don't know who went in Wainwright's yawl, some of his hands; Wm. Atterson and Joseph Britton went in Atterson's; don't know who went in Herring's. Went outside to the point of the beach .. Expects they went there to get coffee, as they were talking about it. I stayed by the yawl when we got to the place, while James Stewart brought a bag of coffee. Witness went for one, met Noah Flynn, and took his. Don't know where the coffee came from, nor who took it from the vessel. Took nothing else. Laid there for an hour. Saw some coffee in Wainwright's boat—four or five bags. There was a barrel of mackerel in the skiff. The boats were launched from the beach; and then witness and others went on board the sloop "New Jersey," taking with them nothing else but the two bags of coffee and the anchor. These things were taken to New York, and put on board the "Daniel Rogers," by captain Hulsehart's orders , in order to be sent to Cedar Creek. Witness and Stewart were promised by prisoner half of what was taken. Ephriam Atterson's sloop lay near the *New Jersey*—she was called "*the Citizen.*" Captain Hatch came on board the *New-Jersey* when her mainsail was being hoisted. Young John Allen and someone else was with him. Asked if he came on board to search, to which captain Hatch replied he had. Hulsehart answered, he might search and welcome.

Witness and H. Cornelius stole the jib out of the corner of the tent. Don't' know where it is now; it was carried to the Sand Hills, toward Herring's.

Daniel Rogers examined. - The prisoner asked him if he would take some things for him to Cedar Creek, a small anchor and two bags of coffee, and they were put on board.

Two other witnesses were called to speak to the character of the boy Everingham. They said he did not bear a good character in the neighborhood in which he lived, being given to telling lies.

Friday, Oct. 9

The District Attorney summed up the case. He remarked that although the testimony of an accomplice should be looked at with suspicion, yet where there was no doubt that the individual who stood charged with an offense against the laws, was engaged in the commission of the crime, then a jury could resort to the testimony of an accomplice for the purpose of showing what particular part he took in it. With regard to the sympathy which was asked in behalf of the prisoner, he had no right to expect any if guilty of the charge.

Judge Baldwin charged the jury in a very lucid and perspicuous manner - explaining the meaning of acts of congress in relation to shoals, banks, & for the purpose of showing that the court had jurisdiction over this matter, and the indictment had been properly framed.

The jury retired, and after an absence of an hour returned into the court with a verdict of guilty on the fifth count of each indictment and not guilty on the remainder.

Friday, Oct.9

Job Platt, Isaac Allen and Abraham Allen were tried for stealing from the *Henry Franklin*, on the 19th of November 1834; five barrels of mackerel of the value of twenty dollars, the property of a person or persons unknown.

The facts of the case are briefly these; One the night of the 18th November last, the schooner *Henry Franklin* was driven by stress of weather, on a bank or shore near Barnegat Inlet, and was obliged to run on a beach, where she lay between high and low water mark. On the evening of the 20th a larger number of persons were collected at a tavern in the neighborhood and they moved down to the scene of plunder, destroyed some of the articles, and removed as many as they could. To do this it was necessary to break open the hatches and a quantity of mackerel was taken off and destroyed. Evidence was added to show that all the parties were concerned in the transaction. Verdict not yet returned at the time of the printing.

Pirate Trial outcome;

The preceding transcript is a bit hard to follow, but to sum up the case, men were indicted for stealing and plundering; an anchor, coffee, mackerel and boxes of soap. Six men were convicted and sentenced to imprisonments, varying from three months to four and a half years and fined. Charges of Piracy were never proven but the men were convicted of stealing and plundering. A suspected ring-leader William Platt, who was a Justice of the Peace, avoided imprisonment by escaping to unknown distant land. Platt had posted $4,000 to bond prior to trial and his money was declared forfeited.

This information comes from - *New Jersey History*, a book published by the New Jersey Historical Society in 1877.

It appears that many others were originally implicated but once the claims of the insurance company were settled, the District Attorney entered "Nolle Prosequi." This latin legal phrase meant he was unwilling to pursue the remaining indictments. Many of those who were not prosecuted may have been let-go in exchange for their testimony against the others.

The whole case had a lasting impression on the community and later in 1835 another storm drove the passenger ship "*Sovereign*" ashore where survivors were robbed. The Newark Sentinel of Freedom Newspaper ran the headline; "New Jersey Land Pirates Again!"

This was actually an unrelated incident where crew of this ship were implicated. The newspaper had to quickly print a retraction.

Island of St. Michaels, February 1st 1852
SHIPWRECK LETTER
An actual first hand account of a shipwreck.

Dear Mother,

I now take this opportunity to write to you to inform you that I am at present well, but in rather sad condition, but must do the best we can. We are ship wrecked. We left New York on 13th December. We had heavy winds from the west and north west and heavy snow squalls until the 23rd, 24 & 25th.

We were scudding before the wind under bare poles and on the morning of the 25th, being Christmas day, blowing a perfect hurricane about three o'clock shipped at sea. Filled the cabin part full of water, carrying away the stove lashings and furniture of the cabin: also tearing the state room partitions, making a complete ruin at four o'clock.

All hands employed in saving the things and bailing the water out of the cabin.

Captain and one man at the wheel shipped another dreadful heavy sea, filling the cabin full of water, breaking the main boom, and washing our dear and much loved captain over-board and at the same time shifting our deck load to lea-ward, leaving our vessel on the bean end first.

We tried to get the storm to try sail on her to bring her head to, but as there was no time to lose she kept going slowly down then we cut away her masts. Her house, the top of it was all underwater but oh, the most heart rending when we cut the mast away.

They cut them and she came up the foremast fell in three pieces and as it gave away the mate started to run aft to clear the falling mast. It fell on him and killed him, poor soul.

It mangled him so that he survived but ten or fifteen minutes. He was hurt so badly that he never spoke, only gave a few groans and died in the arms of me and Rueben.

This happened about six o'clock in the morning. We kept him until about 5 o'clock P.M. We could keep him no longer owing to the bad weather. We served the body up in blankets and one of the passengers read prayers and also the funeral ceremony used on such occasions, and the body of Mr. George L. Williams was committed to the great deep; to us a last and long farewell.

Oh Mother, you do not know what it is to part with our friends and shipmates at sea. We cannot tell you our feelings on these occasions, but it was considerable better for us as one of the crew understood navigation a little so as fortune proved we made the Island of St. Michaels after being rolled and driven to and fro by the sea and gales as we could not rig sail to go only when the wind was fair and when it was ahead.

We had to lay to five, six, seven and eight days at a time. Our shipwreck took place on the 25th of December and we got no assistance until the 25th of January.

We only saw four vessels and they were to far off to see us.

I think there is better land ahead for us. We have been moored here at anchor and I have been ashore today as it is Sunday and rode out in the country about four miles. I shall try to get the American council to send me, Rueben home, if I can, for we want to come, but if he won't let us, we shall have to stay until we get word from the owners and we shall know what to do.

If I am spared to get there you need not have trouble concerning my going to sea, for I shall seek some other employment. But of all places for fruit this exceeds all the known world- oranges, bananas, sweet lemons, grapes and small fruits of all kinds.

We have two Sundays in this country, one for the king, the other for church Sunday!

We are unloading the vessel and then tow her in the basin if there is room. If not we will have to take her to a harbor called the Isle of France, fifteen miles from this seafront. We lay moored off the port. But it is like laying anchored outside of the beach. The cargo is took on shore in boats and when it is safe to stay on board, we leave the vessel and go on shore, and when weather permits, come on board again.

The American council has written to the owners to have them consent to what is best to do with her, for if they sell her here she will not bring over two or three hundred dollars and she is worth eight or nine thousand dollars.

I went on shore today and talked with the council about a passage home. He said that he would send us if he could and if we do start we won't get to New York until about the middle of March. But don't fail in sending me a letter here and when you write direct your letter to Island of St. Michael,

Port Degarda, care of Mr. Maning, British Hotel.

It is Tuesday morning. We are all well at present and hope these few lines may find you in same state of health.

We have nothing to do with the cargo. It is easy time now.

Give my love to all my friends. Rueben send his love to all of you and wants to see you all again.

No more at present but still remain your true son. Goodbye father, mother, sister and brother. This to all. Don't grieve for me. I am doing well.

A.J. Evernham

Andrew Jackson Evernham was the son of Isaac and Emeline (Hall) Evernham of Monmouth County, New Jersey. He lived through this incident and married 3 years later to Hannah Grant. They raised at least two of their four children in Iowa. According to his obituary, he was a former sea captain and died at age 55. It's possible that he served in the military during the civil war since his headstone has a GAR marker. *"Grand Army of the Republic"*

This 1803 New York Advertisement was likely from John Everingham of Charleston, S.C.
(who later owned the ship; *Saucy Jack*)

A famous privateer schooner named "Saucy Jack"

A Legal Pirate Ship

Privateers were captains of merchant ships that had been legally sanctioned by the U.S. Government to attack and capture enemy ships during times of war. American privateers had played a role in the American Revolution, and War of 1812. The United States Constitution contains a provision for authorizing privateers. In the War of 1812 American privateers played a major role, as armed merchant ships sailing from American ports attacked, seized, or destroyed many British merchant ships. The American privateers actually did much more damage to British shipping than the U.S. Navy, which was greatly outnumbered and outgunned by Britain's Royal Navy.

The Privateer Schooner named "*SAUCY JACK*" had a 90 foot deck, 24 foot beam, and displaced 170 tons. It boasted from 6 to 13 guns at various times throughout the War of 1812.

This Charleston, South Carolina based privateer was launched with fanfare on Aug. 6, 1812 by the Pritchard and Shrewbury yard on the Cooper river under Capt. Thos. Jervey. The American Watchman Newspaper of Wilmington, Delaware recorded the launch of the beautiful privateer ship *Saucy Jack* and said it was ready for sea at Charleston. By far the most successful of the privateers that sailed for Charleston in the war of 1812, the 6 to 13 gun schooner was painted black with a white streak along her side to distinguish her. Her first impressive capture was the brig *William Rathbone* which had fourteen guns and a cargo worth 40,000 pounds. That ship was intercepted and taken by another en-route to Charleston. One capture of the *Saucy Jack* was a little sloop known as *Brothers*. It made it back to Charleston. After one cruise with 3 captured vessels, Capt. Peter Sicard took command on October 31st for the second cruise where 4 vessels were captured. In December 1812, in company with the privateer known as *Two Brothers* of New Orleans, the *Saucy Jack* took the brig *Antrim*. The two privateers, still in company on January 19th, also took the ship *Mentor*. Both prizes reached New Orleans safely and were reported worth about $150,000. In September, 1812, Sicard brought two prizes (captured vessels) into St. Mary's, Georgia, and then headed to Charleston. On the way home she encountered the Spanish ship *LaVicente* which had ten long-guns and forty men who mistakenly started an attack. The fight was stopped and only two men were wounded. The *Saucy Jack* reached Charleston April 12, 1813. In Charleston Sicard left the *Saucy Jack* and command was given to it's most renown Captain **John P. Chazal** in April, 1813. Among the 150 crewmen, he brought with him; Lt. Dale Carr, second Lieutenant Lewis Jantzen and ship's surgeon, Dr. James McBride with him. Chazal, Jantzen & McBride had formerly led the crew of the *Defiance*. Captain Chazal stayed with this command until the war's end in January, 1815.

The Saucy Jack and Chazal were a good pairing that proved to be profitable for it's Charleston based owner, merchant **John Everingham**. From 1800 to 1830 Census data of Charleston, South Carolina shows us that John Everingham and wife Rebecca resided there. City directories tell us that John was a merchant and court records indicate that he owned, or co-owned other ships. As an example; in an 1810 court case about the schooner *Doris*, testimony suggested that John Everingham of Charleston was the sole owner of that ship. John Everingham was a co-signer (with Capt. Chazal & Dr. McBride) in 1816 for the disability paperwork of one of the seaman, John Baker of the *Saucy Jack*. ———————→
The American Neptune, Peabody Museum of Salem notes that the *Saucy Jack* was owned by John Everingham of Charleston. We know, from cemetery records, that John died in 1831.

Argus Press, Albany, New York, November 1814

SAUCY JACK'S CRUIZE.

Arrived, yesterday, at this port, the fine fast sailing privateer schooner *Saucy Jack*, John P. Chazel commander, from a cruise of 70 days—with her prize the British schooner Jane, with rum, sugar, shrub, &c. The Saucy Jack has had a very severe engagement with a bomb ship, in which she lost 8 men killed and 15 wounded, among the latter is Mr. Johnson her first Lieutenant. She has a full cargo of British dry goods taken out of a large ship she had captured bound to Aux Cayes from Greenock. The probable value of the goods brought in, is said to be between seventy and eighty thousand dollars. The Saucy Jack has also brought in twenty prisoners, and paroled three times that number during her cruize.—*Sav. paper.*

Much is known about the *Saucy Jack* from various records of the exploits of the vessel found in many American and English history books and war records. It was also featured in local newspapers (*shown above*). A survivor of a captured ship reported in January 1814 - "*we were boarded, she proved to be the privateer schooner Saucy Jack, Capt. John P. Chazel, on a cruise, 5 weeks out from Savannah. She had captured several prizes among which was the brig Sir John Sherbrooke, which had been boarded the same morning.*"

The *Saucy Jack* of Charleston, passed through several heated, severe combats. On April 30, 1814, in the windward passage between Cuba and Santo Domingo, she met the British ship *Pelham*, a large vessel of five hundred and forty tons, and having a compliment of ten guns. *Pelham* was bound from London to Port au Prince. The *Pelham* fought well, and the action reportedly lasted two hours at the end of which she was boarded. English records say that the Pelham's crew of forty men were overpowered by numbers, but resisted with a resolve that commanded the admiration of the victors.

Both vessels reached Charleston safely, and the *Saucy Jack* at once set out again.

<u>Captain Chazal's log on the taking of the *Pelham*</u>:
"In the act of boarding, Stephen Dunham, one of our seamen, was shot dead and our First Lieutenant, Dale Carr, mortally wounded while fighting on the enemy's deck. At the same time our second Lieutenant Lewis Jantzen and John St. Amand, Lieutenant of Marines, were severely wounded, together with 7 of our men. Making our loss 2 killed and nine wounded, 8 of which badly. On board the *Pelham* there were 4 killed and 11 wounded; among the latter, the Captain and his Chief Mate (since died)."

When they reached Charleston on May 20th the City Gazette had this to say;
"*We hardly remember to have seen a finer ship than the Pelham; she is 540 tons, coppered to the bends, mounts ten 12-pound cannonades and long 6's, and had a compliment of from 35 to 40 men. Her cabin is hung round with a great variety of large and elegant naval prints in rich gilt frames*."

The *Jack* had also taken a pipe organ and piano from the *Pelham*. It isn't hard to imagine the loud singing and celebratory atmospheres generated by musical accompaniment aboard the 24 by 90 foot deck of the privateer vessel. Scenes of singing straight from modern-day pirate movies likely couldn't compare to the crew of over 130 celebrating privateers! The famed *Saucy Jack* and it's regularly reported success' made seamen eager to serve aboard her. On July 21, 1814 the following notice appeared in a Charleston Newspaper;
"*The privateer schooner Saucy Jack opened a rendezvous yesterday at 11 o'clock, for the enlistment of her crew. Before 5 P.M. one hundred and thirty able-bodied seamen were shipped in six hours and ready to engage in the glories and dangers of an Atlantic cruise*."

On August 9th she brought the ship *Hoppett* and the brig *Eliza* both with cargo of cotton to Savannah, Georgia. *Saucy Jack* also took the *Kingston Packet* which had a small brass gun on board. On October 31, 1814, about 1 am, being then off Cape Tiburon at the west end of Haiti, she sighted two vessels standing to the westward. Chase was made

and an hour later the privateer opened fire. The strangers replied at the same time shortening sail, which slowed them down. This had to look ominous but the *Saucy Jack* continued onward perhaps thinking that the ships felt safe having their attacker outnumbered. At 6am, having arrived within a few hundred yards, the enemy were seen to be well armed but appeared not to be well manned, so they continued. It was discovered that one ship contained sixteen guns and the other eighteen, but this still did not deter the attackers. At seven, daylight properly lit the area, and the *Saucy Jack* began an engagement with the nearer ship and ten minutes later ran alongside her, ready to board. At this point, she was found to be full of British soldiers!

Captain Chazal broke off their attack quickly, and began a rare retreat. They were followed by an incessant fire of ship's guns and musketry. This awkward escape which brought the chance of a disabling shot, mowing down of crew and consequent capture, lasted an hour. The British pursued for three miles but finally, the speed of the schooner Jack took her out of range. In this narrow escape, eight men were killed and fifteen wounded. To add, two cannon shots had hit the hull and rigging was shot up. It was afterwards ascertained that her opponent was captain Price aboard the British ship **Volcano**, a bomb-ship. It was convoying the transport ship *Golden Fleece*. On board the *Volcano* and escorted ship were <u>two hundred and fifty</u> musket armed troops. The *Volcano* lost an officer and two men killed, and two wounded. The Jack's now first Lieutenant Jantzen was wounded, having recently recovered after taking the *Pelham*. The event was a narrow escape for the privateer and proved that under even the most awkward circumstances, the *Saucy Jack* could give as well as take.

Savannah was a regular return port and was a safe haven for the Jack and her crew. While there on Sept. 20, 1814, the Jack's fore-mast was struck by lightening and the bolt exited out the stern. After repairs, she continued in the West Indies and on November 6th, She had captured eight prizes, for one of which, the ship *Amelia*, she had to fight vigorously, killing four and wounding five of the enemy, while herself sustaining a loss of one killed and one wounded. Chazal decided to take the most valuable cargo aboard which was lucky, because a few days later, *Amelia* had to be abandoned as it burned. On November 28 she arrived at Savannah with the captured schooner *Jane* filled with rum, sugar, as well as dry goods from the *Amelia*. That total prize was said to be worth between seventy and eighty thousand dollars.

The *Saucy Jack* was among the most successful privateer ships of the south. In Georgia and South Carolina, the *Saucy Jack* was a source of local pride. She returned to Charleston on New Year's Eve. News of the peace reached Charleston in February of 1815, and the Jack then began work as a merchant ship. Her captures, engagements with foreign ships, and narrow escapes were unparalleled with any Southern privateer.

The unlucky privateer ship; The General Armstrong

There was another famous brig based out of New York, named General Armstrong and although this ship with the same name likely had it's own exploits and adventures, it is overshadowed by it's more famous namesake. This *General Armstrong* was owned by John Sinclair and John Everingham. Everingham was also the owner of the celebrated privateer vessel *Saucy Jack*. Sinclair was the son of Henry Sinclair of Gloucester, Virginia. John Everingham was a shipping merchant from Charleston and was likely a silent partner or owned a cut in the prizes won by the *General Armstrong*. His profits were few compared to other ships he owned.

The *General Armstrong* was 205 tons, had 16 guns and carried a crew of from 60 to 120 men. She was captained by part-owner John Sinclair. She set out to sea on Christmas Eve of 1812. The City Gazette and Commercial Daily Advertiser gave her this sendoff in a December issue; "*After thundering the notes of preparation for several months, the privateer ship General Armstrong, captain Sinclair, has put to sea. If the length of her cruize equals that of her fitting out, she must be a fortunate sailor if not a swift one. We wish her much success and fewer rebuffs at sea than she has met on shore,.. May she return with rich prizes and lawful ones, and may her crew be enabled another year to enjoy*

a merry Christmas." Instead of doing her hunting in the British West Indies, her captain took her across the Atlantic to a French port. From this time on, she had much happen that could be categorized as unlucky. She lost her stern-boat while being chased by a British frigate. Her only British prize was the brig *Tartar* with a hundred and sixty puncheons of rum. It's known that she later captured a brig called *Stag*, a Schooner named *Menange*, and won a fight against a sloop with 6 guns in a four hour battle. Sometimes known as The *unlucky General Armstrong*, this vessel accumulated many serious troubles involving court cases, murder and mutiny. The *General Armstrong* was likely the only active Charleston privateer not schooner rigged, being almost always spoken of as a ship.

According to a 1813 court case argued in the U.S. Circuit Courts, reference to the seizure of the ship named *Matilda*, The President's commission to the private armed ship called *General Armstrong* was in usual form the 23rd November, 1812. The ship was also stated to belong to **John Everingham** and John Sinclair; and authority was given to John Sinclair, captain, and David Pearce, lieutenant of said ship, and the officers and crew thereof to subdue and take any British vessel. John Sinclair was further authorized to detain, seize, and take all vessels and effects, to whomsoever belonging, which shall be liable according to the law of nations and the rights of the United States as a power at war. The *Matilda* was said to be en-route to England and was pirated by the *General Armstrong*, or by her mutinous crew. According to this case, Captain John Sinclair testified that on March 18th he had been dispossessed of the command of the ship by William Livingston and other officers and crew. John Everingham is mentioned a couple of times in this court case but lucky for him, did not seem to be a part of the action.

MUTINY aboard the General Armstrong!

On March 18th, 1813, a letter was handed to Captain Sinclair on board the General Armstrong, it involved warning him that the crew was very upset as supplies were running low. "*We trust you will shape our course towards the United States, or if you think we can get to France before our provisions be out, go thither; in so doing we are willing and at all times ready to obey your commands.*" ... it was signed by sixty-three persons... At some point, Captain Sinclair was shut-up in his cabin and William Livingston took charge of the ship. By mid April of 1813 the *General Armstrong* arrived in port at Wilmington, North Carolina with John Sinclair, Esquire reporting to local authorities of a Mutiny. - "*I have divided the mutineers in number sixty one on-board.*" A captain's word was law aboard his vessel. Mutiny, and revolts against captains were rare because they were dealt with quickly and severely. But this was a unique situation that was not handled the usual way. Sailing master Thomas N. Gautier took the accused crew into custody and held them on-board gunboats.

The taking of the *Matilda* case appealed to the Circuit Court, and was presided over by Chief Justice John Marshall. He ordered that the *Matilda* be released to her owners and added; "*Taking the case as it stands, it appears a little awkward for the United States to sanction an act that necessarily springs from another which they have said, by the legislature, shall be punished by death. The crew in a state of mutiny made the capture: mutiny is punished with death.*" He seemed to say that the prisoners should be put to death. However, luckily for the crew, the case was being handled by the military.

In the case of the mutineers aboard the *Genearal Armstrong*, there were not enough commissioned naval officers available to hold a court-marshal, and before Secretary of the Navy Jones could get legal advice, a misunderstanding occurred which resulted in a shooting death and the start of another trial. One night on his way to shore Captain Oliver, who was for the time-being, caretaker of the *General Armstrong*, was hailed by a patrolling guard-boat. He refused to obey an order to come alongside and in the altercation, was shot and killed. The shooter and superior officer were charged with murder but were acquitted in a separate trial later. Jones ordered the prisoners from the *Armstrong* released. He based his decision on not wanting to force the prisoners to suffer indefinite incarceration and a lack of naval jurisdiction over pirate offenses. So now the military was saying they didn't have jurisdiction and a civilian Judge had suggested the prisoner's should be put to death. The former crew of the *General Armstrong* were set free. Captain Sin-

clair was furious and sent a lengthy letter to the Secretary of the Navy and the President. He never received any responses. In any case, a mutiny trial never happened which left this ship as one of the only known cases of a crew being arrested for mutiny, where they were all set free, with no trial. Some of the crew made it back to Charleston aboard a whale boat or found work elsewhere.

I have found no record of the General Armstrong serving as a privateer again after this incident.

Midshipmen James Everingham

Many American Everingham's served aboard ships at times of peace and war. Very little is currently known about British Everinghams who may have also served in the sea-life. One such person was James Everingham. In the Naval History of Great Brittan, a book printed in 1859, they discuss battles of the War of 1812. In one battle, two ships named the *Primrose*, and the *Erebus* were on the St. Mary's river when attacked by heavy musketry, the British retreated. When they returned to their post at Cumberland Island, they had 4 killed, and 25 wounded including the two captains; a lieutenant of marines John Fraser, and midshipmen James Everingham and Jonathan Haworth Peel. The group prepared for an attack on Savannah, Georgia. The history of this James Everingham is completely unknown but it appears that he was a British crewman. They had taken Cumberland island as a post just prior to the end of the War of 1812. At this same time in history, Everinghams served aboard American ships attacking the British.

Many boats and ships are known to have been operated by the Everingham & Evernham family over many years in America from before Revolutionary war era to modern times. One such example was the *Petrel* which was a sloop that operated out of New Jersey. It was also built from timber off from Evernham land, by that family. A sloop is a sail boat with a single mast and a fore-and-aft rig. A *sloop* has only one head-sail and if a vessel has two or more head-sails, it is usually termed a *cutter*.

The Petrel was built between 1901 & 1902 in Cedar Grove, Ocean County, New Jersey.

Benjamin Abbitt Evernham (1861-1929) and his son Emmett (1884-1966) are credited for building the Petrel, although other family likely helped.

It was built of oak and cedar lumber that was cut from Ben's property at Cedar Creek, Bayville, Ocean County, New Jersey. The lumber used was cut from the family property then taken to the mill and cut into planks and put out to dry.

Raymond Evernham (1888-1930) Captained the Petrel in various areas including the waters of Barnegat Bay, New Jersey. The photo below shows the Petrel in action.

Photo of brothers Raymond (left) and Emmett (right).

Below is a recreation of Ray's business card:

Sloop Yacht "PETREL"
Capt. RAYMOND EVERNHAM

This Commodious Yacht can be hired by the Day, Week or Month for Sailing or Fishing in any part of Barnegat Bay. Cooking and Sleeping Accommodations. $6.00 a day or night for party of six; $1.00 for each one additional; $25 for three days; $50 per week.

PO, SEA SIDE PARK, N.J.
Telegraph Address, BARNEGAT PIER, N.J.

Photos used courtesy of Earle Evernham

The Rebecca Everingham River Steamboat

American boats and ships sailed the east coast with Everingham crew and captains. Branches of our family operated sea-related business and trade out of New Jersey and New York. From the time of the American Revolution, an Everingham family also flourished in the south. It is believed by some family historians that an Everingham privateer (a *Government sanctioned pirate*) in the 1700's made his riches and moved his family to Georgia or the Carolina's. This may be the origins of the southern U.S. Everinghams.

The earliest census data shows a John Everingham living in South Carolina by 1800. A Thomas Everingham married Mary Shadwick in Georgia in 1795. A John Everingham of Georgia married Sarah Barnard. Their daughter was Rebecca Barnard Everingham, born about 1819. It was this Rebecca that the somewhat famous riverboat was named after.

Rebecca Barnard Everingham married Colonel William Morrill Wadley in November of 1840. Mr. Wadley was an employee of the Central Railroad of Georgia. In 1857 he moved his family to take a job managing the Vicksburg, Shreveport and Texas Railroad. In 1861 William M. Wadley was appointed Confederate superintendent of the railroads and in 1864 superintendent of railroad car work. After the civil war, the family moved to Georgia where William became the head of the Georgia Central Railroad in 1866. In 1873 the family moved to a large plantation, "*Great Hill Place*" near Bolingbroke, Monroe County, Georgia. By 1880 when the steamboat "*Rebecca Everingham*" was launched, the Wadley family was a very wealthy and influential family.

Before railroads and automobiles, America's rivers served as the nation's highways for leisurely travel and movement of merchandise to markets. Steam boating was a lucrative industry in the United States for almost 150 years. Steamboat designs varied, and included side-wheel and stern-wheel paddlers, as well as powerful and majestic passenger vessels and heavily loaded cargo boats.

The Rebecca Everingham was a sternwheeler that was both a cargo and luxury passenger boat.

Rivalries between steamboat pilots led to races that often had disastrous results. In the first 40 years of steamboats it was estimated that 500 vessels were lost, taking with them nearly 4,000 lives. Because of the many dangers of river travel and accidents, the average life-span of a steamboat was only four to five years. The advent of efficient automobiles and transcontinental railroads, led to the decline of the steamboat era. By the 1950s, riverboats had become relics of the past. The Rebecca Everingham was in service from 1880 until April 3rd of 1884.

According to the weekly Gleaner, a New York newspaper, the headline read "**A River Horror Burning of a Southern Steamer with Loss of Life**." They reported that on April 3, 1884, people were aroused from sleep to meet death by fire or risk the dark unknown waters. The steamer Rebecca Everingham burned on the Chattahoochee river, at Fitzgerald's plantation, a few miles above Florence, Alabama. In the early hours the fire broke out and many lives were lost.

At about 4 A.M. the engineer on watch rang an alarm signal to the pilot, who called to the officers on watch and asked if he must go to the shore when he was at once ordered to do so. The pilot signaled to the engineer to work for the shore, but got no response. He then headed the boat for the Georgia side, and the momentum she had, carried her almost to the banks. The pilot on watch ordered his teen son, Frank Lapham, to jump overboard with a rope and swim ashore and tie-up the boat to a tree. The boy sprang into the river, struck for the shore, reached it safely and tied the boat up. In the meantime the fire alarm was rung by Pilot George Lapham, and the passengers aroused from their sleep to find the boat in flames. All was confusion and disorder. By all accounts, the officers of the boat were heroic in the performance of their duty. Nearly all of crew were wounded or burnt. The flames wrapped the boat in their fiery embrace.

Those known to be lost in the fire are as follows; W.L. Kennedy of Spring Hill, Alabama., the deputy sheriff of Barbour county; Mrs. Avart of Cuthbert, Georgia; Miss Simpson of Fort Gaines, Georgia.; J.B. Yates of Bainbridge; two white men

---

The Fredonia Censor
Wednesday, April 9, 1884

A Steamboat Horror Columbus, Ga., April 3 - The steamer Rebecca Everingham, Captain George Whiteside, burned to the water's edge at Fitzgerald Landing on the Chattahoochee river, 140 miles below this city. The fire originated in the stern of the steamer, and is thought from an electric lamp spark. Some passengers were saved and escaped in their night clothes. The boat was valued at $24,000 and is a total loss with no insurance. There were sixteen cabin passengers and nine deck pasengers on board. The steamer belonged to the Central Line and plied the Chattahoochee river between that city and Apalachacola Bay. A Macon dispatch says that of thirty passengers, thirteen are dead and missing. Capt. George H. Whiteside was painfully burned. all the officers did their duty. The conduct of Pilot George Lapham and son, a lad of 14 years, is especially commended. They remained on board and materially assisted in landing the passengers.

---

whose names were unknown; Julia Adams, a colored chambermaid; Dolph Thomas, a colored fireman; Randal Singer and Aaz Stevens, colored deck hands; Bob Griffin, a colored, stevedore and a colored woman and child, names unknown.

Captain G.B. Whiteside was severely burned on the face, head, and hands, E.D. Williams of Langrange, Georgia was thought to be fatally burned. J.T. Carey, assistant engineer, was painfully burned.

There were 307 bales of cotton aboard the steamer, 216 of which were taken on at Eufaula. She was made fast to the shore by two hawsers, which were finally burnt. She remained tied to the bank about forty-five minutes, when her moorings burned and the wreck floated out in the stream, drifted about one hundred yards, careened and sunk. The fire broke out among the cotton just aft mid-ship. It is not known how it originated.

Gun Accidents;

Accidentally shot with a 38.

In Buffalo, New York, April 1904, an Everingham man was shot in the face by accident late one night. As New York newspaper; The Wyoming County Times reported, *"A serious accident happened at James Mahoney's saloon shortly after midnight."* This particular newspaper spelled his name *"Ervingham."* They further reported - Louis Evringham is under a doctor's care with a bullet in his throat and Edward Keyes is out on $1,000 bail with a charge of assault in the first degree. This was a case of carelessness, not a criminal attack. The police had no doubt that the shooting was accidental. Keyes, Ervingham and Norton Slayton were chatting in the kitchen when Keyes drew a 38-calibre revolver to show the other men. As he was about to hand it to Ervingham, the gun went off and the bullet struck Ervingham in the mouth, knocking out two teeth and lodging in his throat. Sergeant L.L. Brown and Patrolman H. Terhorst arrested Keyes. By other reports the wound was not fatal but quite serious.

Louis Guy Everingham had married Gertrude Cook in 1898 and had two children by 1904. Louis lived through a horrific ordeal but was able to lead a normal life afterwards. Later in life, he had two more children and retired to Florida in his later years.

War hero loses his young son to a shooting accident

Corporal John B. Everingham was born 1844 in Pennsylvania. His father and brothers had served in the Civil War. John was in the Pennsylvania heavy artillery and fought at the battle of the Wilderness and several other battles including Cold Harbor, Spottsylvania and the capture of Petersburg April 8 1865. He was honorably discharged from the military in 1866. John chose to settle in northern Michigan to start his life and married Miss Anna Tackaberry. He was respected enough that there is an Everingham street in Alba, Michigan, named after him. Anna was also a native of Pennsylvania but came to Michigan with her parents; Joseph and Julia, at a young age. John and Anna's early years were very tough and made worse when their first son Claude and second son William both died at young ages of sickness. In 1885 things looked-up for the couple when their only daughter *"Lura"* was born. In 1888 a son they named *"DeForest"* was born. The family was complete and despite the loss of two children, life was fairly normal for the Everingham four. The family lived between Alba and Wetzell in Mancelona township, Antrim County. By March of 1898, DeForest was a healthy, normal 9 year old boy, but the family was destined again to be rocked by tragedy. The local Mancelona newspaper reported this incident -

"One of the saddest accidents The Hearld has ever been called upon to chronicle occurred at Wetzell Thursday afternoon, by which DeForest Everingham, the only son of Mr. and Mrs. John B. Everingham, lost his life. The accident happened at the house of Mr. F.D. Zimmerman, while the family were away from home. It seems that Mr. Zimmerman's two boys, Ray and Roy, with the Everingham lad - all between 9 and 11 years of age - were playing with a 38-calibre Winchester rifle, when, in some manner the piece was discharged, instantly killing DeForest."

The Antrim County death certificate shows DeForest Everingham died at Mancelona township on March 24, 1898. He was nine years, five months, twelve days old. In November of the following year, John Everingham also passed away. Mrs. Everingham lived until 1918 and their daughter Lura lived until December of 1960. John, Anna, and DeForest are all buried in Alba, Michigan.

Mrs. Joseph Everingham shot, But saved by her corset!

An early 1900's newspaper known as The Silver Springs Signal, ran a story in about 1905, that reported an accidental shooting in New York. Silver Springs is a small community in Wyoming county. The reporter wrote; *"We nearly had a fatality to chronicle this week, with some of the campers in Dr. Randall's grove at Silver Lake, the victims."*

Dr. Reed, a dentist of Perry, New York, who has quite a reputation as a daring automobilist, stopped his machine in the road, up-back of the doctor's cabin, took his rifle and shot at what he thought was a woodchuck in the edge of the grove. The bullet flew wide of the mark and went into the crowd enjoying themselves in the shade. It just grazed the head of Mrs. Fred Stoddard and struck her mother, Mrs. Joe Everingham in the back.

Fortunately it struck a corset steel which stopped the force of the ball, but her back was quite badly bruised.

"It was a very lucky outcome, as it is a wonder that some of the campers were not killed or seriously injured."

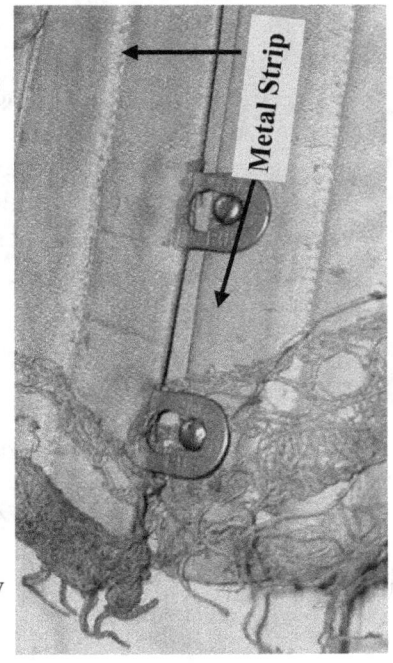

Metal Strip

Mrs. Fred Stoddard, also known as Lottie Belle Everingham, was born in New York in 1885. She was the only daughter of Joseph Everingham and Mary J. Howard. Mrs. Mary J. Howard-Everingham was born in Michigan about 1867 and passed away in 1907 within a couple of years after the shooting. Dr. Reed and this Everingham family of Wyoming County, N.Y. eluded tragedy that day due to the heavy metal design of the common corset in use from 1895 to the early 1900s. It had metal strips along each side where metal studs attached on one side and metal loops on the other. The simple sliding design replaced the old-style lace-up corsets. Luckily for Mrs. Everingham she was wearing the metal style.

Mistook his friend for a deer

Family researchers of the Everingham family of Canada know of the connections between the Lymburner and Everinghams in Ontario. A couple newspaper headlines from 1889 tell of this unfortunate case of mistaken identity.

The Hiram Lymburner in this story was a relative of the Charlotte (Lymburner) and Hiram Everingham family of Haldimand County, Ontario, and also related to James Everingham's wife; Margaret Lymburner of Haldimand, Ontario. James was a brother of Henry, Eugene and Ira Everingham who migrated to Michigan.

Hiram Lymburner was the son of Horace and Mary (Merritt) Lymburner of Ontario. December 5, 1889 the Daily Times of Troy, New York ran a story about Hiram and his friend William Kennedy hunting on December 4th near Owen Sound, Ontario, near where they lived. Kennedy saw what he thought was a deer and fired a shot. The shot struck and killed Hiram instantly. The New York Press ran this headline the same day - **Killed his friend for a deer**. The headline was a bit sensationalized and misleading, but the written account accurately relayed the story;

"While William Kennedy and Hiram Lymburner were hunting today, Kennedy fired at a supposed deer, shooting Lymburner, killing him instantly."

FATAL ACCIDENT

Brooklyn N.Y. Union-Argus, Thursday, Dec 8, 1881

How a man and his double-barreled gun were soon parted. —— Bordentown, N.J. Dec 8, Everinham Disbrow, 32 years of age, was killed near Clarkstown, Monmouth County yesterday. He attempted to blow the powder out of one barrel of his gun when the other barrel exploded, blowing the top of his head off.

This story also ran the next day in the New York Times, and in New Jersey papers including The Red Bank Register, N.J.

Accidents;

6 year old boy tumbles over moving Freight Train & Lives!
**The Syracuse Daily Journal,
Monday, August 13, 1894**

Neighborhood News, Onondaga County, New York - **Fred Everham, the 6-year-old son of W.S. Everham of this place, had a narrow escape from death Sunday.** While standing on the railroad bridge, watching a long freight train on the N.Y.C. passing under him, he suddenly became dizzy and tumbled off, striking on top of the passing train. A number of persons who had seen him fall, rushed to the bridge in time to see the lad roll from a box-car to the ground. He was picked up and carried into Young's barber shop, where Dr.Coe made an examination. Young Everham was badly shaken up but aside from a broken arm and sprained ankle his injuries are not dangerous. The little lad's escape was miraculous.

Minor Car Accident, in 1922
The Norwitch NY, Chenango Union News

Cars driven by Albert Smith of Oxford and W.S. Everham of this city, were in collision at the corner of North Broad and West Side Park on Thursday morning. Mr. Everham's car was slightly damaged.

Serious Car Accident, in 1923
Wyoming County New York Times, September 20, 1923
FORMER WARSAW MAN BREAKS HIP IN AUTOMOBILE ACCIDENT
J. Frank Everingham of LeRoy, a former resident of Warsaw sustained a fractured hip in an automobile accident on the main road between Stafford and LeRoy Saturday afternoon, besides being painfully cut and bruised, P.C. Cornelius of Vick. Ark., received a deep gash on his left arm. Mrs. Everingham and Mrs. C. Oswald Hawken, also of LeRoy were cut and bruised. Mrs. Cornelius, a bride of one

day escaped injury. A third car going west attempted to pass. The third machine hit Everingham's coupe and forced it into Mr. Cornelius' big touring car wrecking both. The driver of the third car turned down a side road and escaped towards Roanoke.

James Frank Everingham was born 1858 in Warsaw, Wyoming County, New York. He went by the name "Frank" At the time of this accident, he was married to Bertha Buell. Frank had two sons; Floyd and Leon. Frank died in LeRoy, NY in 1931.

Bothwell Times, Canada, April 6, 1922
Serious Accident befell Norman Everingham

An almost a fatal accident befell Norman Everingham, assistant lineman for the Urban and Rural Telephone Co., Monday morning he had ascended a pole at the corner of Oak and Peter and was making repairs when the pole broke at the bottom and fell to the ground. By some means, the pole on striking the ground, sprung up, striking Norman with such force on the head that he was unconscious for seven hours. Dr. Graham is in charge, and we are pleased to state that Norman is considerably better, and no serious result is anticipated.

This story is about Norman Wesley Everingham who was born 1901 in Bothwell, Kent, Ontario He married Maria Bordeau in 1930 and had a son later that year, so obviously he fully recovered from this accident. Norman lived until 1965.

Cortland NY Independent Villager, June 30, 1986
Bob Everingham Jr. 36 Dies in Farm Accident

Robert I. Everingham, 36 of Clark Hollow Road, LaFayette, died Wednesday in a farm accident. He graduated from LaFayette Central School, Cornell University and received his master's degree from Indiana University. Mr. Everingham apparently came in contact with electrical equipment on an automatic feed loader he was trying to fix about 15 feet up in the 60 foot silo, State Police and LaFayette fire officials said.

I corresponded with Robert Irwin Everingham Sr., Robert's father in 2003 and he shared information about his family history. Robert said very little about his son and I didn't push him further. It was obviously a very painful topic. He and wife Blanche also had a daughter named Carol. Robert Sr, like his son, was a Cornell alumni. Robert Sr. received the Purple Heart from his Army service during WWII.

Wife of New Jersey Mayor, & A Youth Killed in Crash

The Philadelphia Inquirer, Oct. 31, 1960

City Official also hurt in Accident... The wife of **Mayor Donald G. Everingham**, of Avalon, New Jersey and a Philadelphia youth were killed early Sunday in a head-on automobile crash on the Black Horse Pike, near Weymouth N.J.
Mayor Everingham, 33, was injured critically in the accident.

Dead were Mrs. Gladys Everingham, 32, and Stanley R. Steinbronn Jr., 19. They were pronounced dead at Atlantic City Hospital. Both suffered head injuries.

MAYOR'S NECK BROKEN
Mayor Everingham was admitted to the hospital suffering from a broken neck and internal injuries.

State police of the Mays Landing barracks said the accident occurred at 1:15 a.m. They said Steinbronn, alone in his car, was driving west.
The Everinghams were traveling east with the Mayor operating the car.

Mrs. Everingham and Steinbronn were hurled through the windshields of the cars by the impact.

Mayor Everingham is also director of public safety at Avalon. He was sworn in as Mayor on May 19, 1959 to succeed Edith Greenan.

Mayor Everingham dies from injuries sustained from accident which also killed his wife.
Follow up story, November 3, 1960
Indiana Gazette, PA, Page 29.

Donald G. Everingham, 33, mayor of Avalon, N. J., since 1959, died today in Atlantic City Hospital of injuries suffered Sunday in a two-car collision. Everingham's wife, Gladys, 32, and Stanley R. Steinbronn Jr., 19, of Philadelphia, were killed instantly in the crash on the Black Horse Pike in Weymouth, N.J.

Everingham and his wife were returning from a meeting of the Order of the Eastern Star in Burlington City, N.J., at the time of the crash.

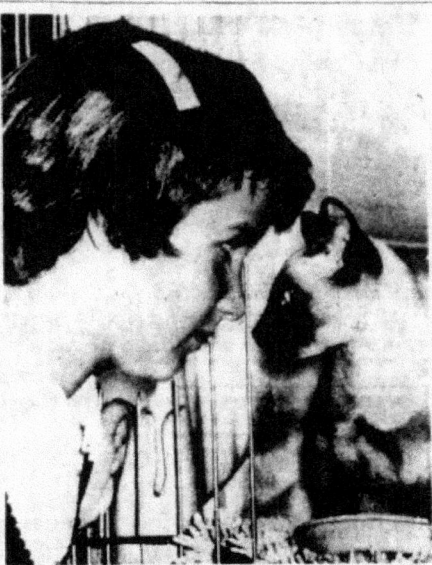

Wife of N. J. Mayor, Youth Killed in Crash

City Official Also Hurt In Accident

The wife of Mayor Donald G Everingham, of Avalon, N J., and a Philadelphia youth were killed early Sunday in a head-on automobile crash on the Black Horse Pike, near Weymouth, N. J.

Mayor Everingham, 33, was injured critically in the accident.

Dead were Mrs. Gladys Everingham, 32, of 219 19th st., Avalon, and Stanley R. Steinbronn, Jr., 19, of 6121 Walker st. They were pronounced dead at Atlantic City Hospital. Both suffered head injuries.

MAYOR'S NECK BROKEN

Mayor Everingham was admitted to the hospital suffering from a broken neck and internal injuries.

State police of the Mays Landing barracks said the accident occurred at 1:15 A. M. They said Steinbronn, alone in his car, was driving west. The Everinghams were traveling east with the Mayor operating their car.

Mrs. Everingham and Steinbronn were hurled through the windshields of the cars by the impact.

EASTERN STAR OFFICIAL

Police Supt. Lloyd C. Riggail, of Avalon, who identified the body of Mrs. Everingham at the hospital, said the couple was returning home after attending a meeting of the Order of Eastern Star in North Jersey. He said Mrs. Everingham was an officer of the organization.

Mayor Everingham also is director of public safety at Avalon. He was sworn in as Mayor on

Tiki, a prize-winning Siamese kitten owned by Mr. and Mrs. Edward Casson, of West Chester, exchanges a keen stare with Carol Anne Staffieri, 8, of 1528 S. Taylor st., at Penn State Cat Club show.

Dateline . . . Delaware Valley U.S.A

PLAIN-CLOTHES detectives and uniformed policemen attached to the Belgrade and Clearfield sts. station are raising a "Barney Martin Fund" to help a fellow policeman meet medical and other expenses growing out of an automobile accident last Aug. 24.

The fund is for Detective Sgt. Bernard Martin, of the east detective division, whose wife, Rose, 30, and three children, Brian, 6, Mary Ellen, 3, and

The World News, Monday, November 27, 1893
"actual newspaper clipping"

STRICKEN ON A CAR PLATFORM.

Secretary Everingham Dies in an Hour from an Attack of Brain Paralysis.

James Everingham Secretary of the Third Avenue Railroad Employees' Association, died suddenly on a Third avenue car yesterday of paralysis of the brain.

He had been at the Harlem Depot and boarded a downtown car. He stood on the rear platform, conversing with Conductor Knapp. At One Hundred and Twenty-fourth street Everingham fell without even a moan into the conductor's arms.

The conductor, assisted by a passenger, dragged the unconscious man into the car and laid him on the seat. The car was hurried back to the depot. Efforts were made to revive him, but unsuccessfully. An ambulance was called, and he was taken to the hospital, where he died an hour later. He leaves a widow and three children. They live at No. 25 East Ninety-fourth street.

Mr. Everingham was forty-seven years old. He was born in Peekskill and was graduated from Eastman College with the class of 1880. He founded and edited the Herald at San Juan, Col. He was for a long time owner and editor of the Peekskill Messenger.

JOSEPH B. EVERHAM
AT LIBERTY FOR NEXT SEASON.
COMEDY OLD MEN AND CHARACTER. Address Pike Theatre Co., Minneapolis, Minn

Early American actor; J.B. Everham was active in theatre from the mid 19th century to very early 1900's. Joseph's great grandfather is thought to be William Everingham of Springfield, Burlington, New Jersey. The strange spelling of the name Everingham changed slightly from family to family prior to the 20th century as the name was often spelled the way it was pronounced.

In Joseph's time, live stage acting in theatre houses, saloons and traveling shows, was the only way to see a show.

Advertisements, announcements and reviews can be found about his performances in many newspapers from the period. The Advertisement (*heading shown at the start of this article*) is from a New York newspaper in early August of 1900. This was late in Joseph's career. As you can see from his ad, he played "*comedy, old men and character acting.*"

In those days, actors didn't have television and movies to get global face recognition, they relied on newspaper ads and had to advertise for their services for live theatre shows.

An article in the New York Dramatic Mirror in 1879 tells of "*then famous*" comedian John Dillon. It states that Dillon had a great hit in a comedy called **Bumps**, which was written by Joseph B. Everham. At that time, Joseph was the stage manager of Blaisdell's acting co. From this article we also know that J. B Everham was a writer, stage manager and comedic actor. Reviews of Bumps explain that is was hilarious - "*the climax of absurdity erupts as Dillon is about to take off his vest to shred it and screams are heard from the ladies on stage, as the curtain drops while the audience is in convulsions of merriment.*" There is little doubt that J.B. was a funny actor and comedian.

A tabloid story appears *on the next page* about Joseph's divorce in 1882 which attempts to tie him to actress Octavia Allen, *shown below*. No proof of any real relationship with Ms. Allen was ever proven but they did act together several times.

19th century American actress "Octavia Allen" was brought into a scandal in 1882 when adultery was alleged with J.B. Everham.

Shocking News

A Early American Actor's divorce
A 19th century tabloid story

Joseph Barras Everham and wife Louisa Kohler were early American actors. They married about 1855 in Baltimore, Maryland. Joseph and Louisa had eight children. I believe that Louisa had a very short acting career. Very little is known about her career but quite a bit can be found about him. In the 1867 city directory of Philadelphia, PA, he is listed as a comedian. Although comedians became well known by the 20th century, it was a somewhat rare profession distinction in 1867. In other places he is noted as a "comedic actor."

The Salt Lake Daily Herald, Utah, December 2, 1882 ran this headline; **Divorce-Libel,** Chicago. "*Some days ago, Mrs. Louisa Everham, wife of J.B. Everham, actor, brought suit for divorce, alleging adultry with Octavia Allen, widow of the late D.R. Allen. Today Mrs. Allen brought suit against Mrs. Everham damages being laid at $10,000.*"

According to the New York Clipper, December 9, 1882, "*The wife of J. B. Everham the actor, now in Chicago, the other day brought suit for divorce against him and named Mrs. Allen, of the profession, in the complaint as correspondent. Now Mrs. Allen brings a suit against Mrs. Everham for ten thousand dollars. It will be a pleasure to us to hear not only that Mrs. Allen is entitled to the damages claimed, but also that the wife of an actor has so much money.*" - much of this article was unfortunately hard to decipher due to the transcription coming from an rough scan of the paper.

The story is reported again and reprinted in North Dakota, Minnesota, New York, California and other states, this likely means that Joseph or Octavia may have been well-known actors.

On May 19, 1883, The Sacramento Daily Record -Union newspaper reported... "*Judge Gardner, of Chicago, has entered his decree in the seperate-maintenance suit of Louisa Everham, actress, against Joseph B. Everham, actor, and ordered him to pay her $65 a month alimony until further orders of the Court.*"

This is a large amount when you consider that in 1880 the average carpenter or blacksmith earned about $60 per month and by 1890 they earned around $70, while general labor workers earned about $32/month in 1880 and $36/month by 1890. By comparison, you can see how this $65 per month in alimony in 1883 was substantial.

J.B. Everham continued to act throughout the 19th century. In 1886 Joseph took a role alongside Octavia Allen in a comedy production called "*The Woman Hater*". It was said that the acting was excellent. Mr. Everham and Ms. Allen appeared together in several shows but I do not believe that anything has ever been found definitively linking them as a couple. In 1897 the Saint Paul Globe in Minnesota reported a show at the Metropolitan opera house. J.B. Everham is described as *a comedian of the old school, whose success upon the stage in roles of comic nature has been quite pronounced. The role of Theodore Bender, the chief mirth-provoker was entrusted to a new member of the company, J.B. Everham, and most happily so entrusted. Mr. Everham is an excellent comedian. His methods are those of the artist. He is buoyant, not boisterous. His laughter is contagious, his expression genial, his demeanor unassuming.*

Actress Octavia Allen's obituary in the New York Hearld stated; "*Octavia Allen, well known divorced actress, died in July, 1893 at age 53.*"

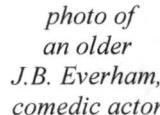

photo of an older J.B. Everham, comedic actor

Billy Rose Theatre Division, The New York Public Library.

A close-call in the Civil War

The Western Reserve Chronicle, Trumbull Co. Ohio
Wednesday, August 24, 1864

Close call as Rebel musket shot splits the scalp of Henry Everingham during combat

From the 13th & 14th Ohio Battery - battling 2 miles from Atlanta, GA *"describes battles of this unit during the Civil War"*... The wounded were Corp. Aaron P. Cox of Mesopotamia, severe in the foot. Privates Seymour P. Jones of Ashtabula Co., in leg, severe; Henry B. Lane of Ashtabula Co., leg amputated; Warren S. Reynolds of Mesopotamia, leg and side, severe. Corporal McCord was scratched on the knee by a passing ball and private Henry Everingham has a furious cut through his hair, from the forehead to the crown, which was certainly close enough. The enemy lost between six and seven hundred which were buried by our men the next day. We also captured about two hundred prisoners.

Private Henry Everingham of the 13th Independent Battery, Light Artillery of Ohio is noted in other sources. In a book that includes this incident, he was said to have continued to man his gun after a wound of a rebel ball that skimmed his head, carrying away the hair and scalp from forehead to crown. He had six children prior to the war and another born after the war. He lived until October 6, 1908 and is buried in Logan County, Ohio.

The sad story of Charles Everingham,
The Auburn Bulletin, N.Y., August 10, 1891

A recruit for the asylum

"Charles Everingham was brought to the insane asylum from the Onondaga county penitentiary by Deputy Sheriff John C. Kratz Saturday afternoon. Everingham was awaiting trial for arson but he was undoubtedly insane when he committed the crime, and violently so, since his confinement."

I have found no follow-up information about the situation involving Charles. This is most likely Charles *"Chet"* Everingham born 1837 of Onondaga, NY. That Charles enlisted in 1862 as a private in the 122nd New York volunteers.
According to the Fayetteville gazette, Charles

Everingham deserted in September of 1863. We don't have knowledge of what Charles went through during his time in the civil war, but apparently it had a huge impact on the rest of his life. His brother John also served in the 122nd. In 1891 Charles Everingham was 54, and listed as a *"miller"* by occupation. This is known from the 1891 New York state census of the state asylum for insane criminals. It was noted that he was received from Onondaga, New York and his residence was Jamesville, N.Y. There is also a story about him drinking heavily in 1892. *(page 13)* The 1892 State census lists his wife and children living without him which makes it very likely that this is the same Charles Everingham. Charles died in 1895 and he is buried at the Walnut Grove cemetery in Jamesville, Onondaga, New York. His wife and another brother are also buried at this cemetery.

FORMER AUBURN WOMAN'S SUICIDE

The Auburn Citizen, N.Y., June 16, 1924

Mrs. Addie Everham plunges into Chenango river near Norwich. The body of Mrs. Addie Everham 55, formerly of Auburn and now of Norwich, was found in the Chenango river a mile and a half south of her home last evening. Relatives believe she committed suicide while suffering from melancholia because of failing health.

The finding of the body terminated an exhaustive search since last Friday when Mrs. Everham disappeared from home. In the hunt for the woman, bloodhounds were used, the dogs losing the trail near the river-bank. This led to the belief that Mrs. Everham had ended her life in the rushing waters. The woman's coat was found near the water's edge and by dragging, the body was recovered.

Mrs. Everham resided in Auburn for a number of years and only the week before Decoration Day was the guest of her sister, Mrs. H.R. Havens of Grant Avenue. For the past she had been suffering from ill health.

Surviving are the husband, the sister of Auburn, a twin brother, Edward Wellington of Warners, and two nieces.

The funeral will be at 2 o'clock Wednesday at Warners, with burial there.

MASKED BANDITS SHOOT PAYMASTER AND DRIVER IN ATTEMPTED ROBBERY

Men, Attacked on Lonely Road Near Mattawan, N. J. Battle Highwaymen Who Seek to Steal Bag Containing $10,000—One Defender May Die of Wound

Special to The Inquirer.

MATTAWAN, N. J. Aug. 10.—Four heavily armed, masked men held up and shot Ray Robinson, paymaster of the New Jersey Brick Company, of Mattawan, N. J., early this afternoon on the lonely road running from the village of Clifford to Mattawan. Robinson was the Middlesex county line and through Cliffwood. It was not until after they had passed through the village of Cliffwood the robbers jumped out from behind a tree, leveled guns at the heads of Robinson and Everham and ordered them to throw up their hands and make no outcry.

Instead of submitting to the command Robinson jumped from his seat to the

Mattawan, N.J., August 10 - *Four heavily armed, masked men held up and shot Ray Robinson, paymaster of the New Jersey Brick Company, of Mattawan, N.J., early this afternoon on the lonely road running from the village of Clifford to Mattawan. Robinson was shot in the head and breast and is not expected to live. His driver, William Everham, was shot in the leg and the rose attached to the buggy in which they were driving was killed by the thieves' bullets. The robbers were scared away by the fight put up by the men, and the payroll of $10,000, which lay in a bag on the seat of the carriage, was saved.*

Robinson and Everham were returning from South Amboy, where the bank at the Middlesex county line and through Cliffwood. It was not until they had passed through the village of Cliffwood the robbers jumped out from behind a tree, leveled guns at the heads of Robinson and Everham and ordered them to throw up their hands and make no outcry.

Instead of submitting to the command, Robinson jumped from his seat to the ground. As he did so, several shots rang out and he fell with a bullet in his forehead over his right eye and another in his right breast. Robinson managed to get himself into a sitting position and grabbed the black handbag of money from the buggy.

When Robinson fell, Everham dropped the reins, seized a revolver and also jumped to the ground. This caused a second volley of shots to be fired. Everham pushed forward towards the bandits and Robinson fell to the ground with a bullet wound in

the forehead. In the fight that ensued the revolver was discharged and Everham fell with a wound in his right leg. From the ground Everham exchanged shots with the bandits, who seemed to be losing heart, and they backed away towards the bushes and disappeared in them. Everham believes he hit one of the men.

It was some minutes before any person arrived to aid the wounded men. When aid did arrive Robinson's first request was to notify the brick company. This was done by telephone and an automobile was sent to the place of the holdup.

After delivering the bag with the company's fund in it, Robinson lapsed into unconsciousness. Robinson was put aboard a train and rushed to a New York hospital in a dying condition. The physicians who examined him asserted that they believed he would not live.

The Philadelphia Enquirer, June 17, 1882
Exact re-print of the newspaper story;

Poor Mr. Everham's dismal experiences of married life.

Charles Everham, under the supposition that his first wife was dead, married a second time in the year 1880. His first wife, Mary Baily, whom he married in 1866, had deserted him. The last time he saw her was in 1869, and he saw nothing of her for five years before his second marriage. Meanwhile he had got a divorce, as he supposed, from his first wife, paying his lawyer $75. But it was not until after he heard his first wife was dead that he married again. A second time he was unfortunate. His second wife, hearing that her predecessor was alive, had him arrested for bigamy, and then brought him up before the desertion court, where he was sued for a divorce from her, and finally prosecuted him on a still more serious charge. At the hearing in the bigamy suit, magistrate List dismissed the case. In the desertion court an order was made on Mr. Everham for the support of his child; but when the second criminal charge came to be tried the defendant took the stand and testified that his second wife's conduct was owing to her interest in another man. He was acquitted.

The pretended lawyer who fleeced him in the divorce suit, which was never terminated, is now said to be driving an express wagon.

St. Paris Era Dispatch, Champaign Co. Ohio, Feb 7, 1901

ANOTHER SUICIDE!
This time it is Cory Everingham the Drayman

Cory Everingham, a popular young man of this place, who lived with his wife on West Main St, took and over-dose of morphine last Monday evening. He and his wife were sitting at the supper table at about 5 o'clock that evening when Everingham suddenly took a paper from his pocket, and unwrapping it swallowed the contents. His wife asked him what it was, and he refused to say. In a few minutes he fell to the floor unconscious. Dr. Hunt and Wolcott were hastily summoned. They could not ascertain what he had taken, therefore could not administer the proper remedy. However, everything was done for the man that was possible but he was past human aid and at 11 o'clock he was pronounced dead.

It was afterwards learned that Everingham had contemplated suicide as he had purchased 10 grains of morphine at one of the local drug stores on Monday afternoon. He had been drinking some that day, and seemed in low spirits. In the afternoon he had went into one of the saloons and invited some of his companions to have a glass of beer after which he started for the door and called back, *"that's the last drink you'll get off me."*

Everingham had been employed for some time by Joseph Gibbs as drayman, and only that day Mr. Gibbs had told him that he would have no work for him for two or three weeks. Brooding over being without employment, probably caused him to commit this rash act.

Cory Leroy Everingham was born in St. Paris, Ohio on September 23, 1874, and died February 4, 1901, aged 26 years, 4 months and 11 days. He was married to Miss Blanche Reams, November 8th 1900. The deceased was an industrious and hard-working young man, and has a host of friends who were grieved to learn that the young man had taken his own life. The family has the sympathy of the entire community.

(same paper, Feb 21, 1901) ... *"Resolution of respect. Whereas the St. Paris Volunteer Fire Department has sustained a loss by death of Cory L. Evernham, and Whereas, it is fitting to pay a tribute to respect to the departed, be it resolved that in the death of Cory L. Evernham, the St. Paris Fire Company has lost a worthy member... E.H. Cline, John Poorman, W.H. Walborn."*

Elderly woman falls and snaps both of her wrists.

Olive Everingham

In February of 1889 Olive Everingham was an elderly woman living with her step-daughter Mary about nine years after Olive's husband Jeremiah Everingham had died. The Everinghams of Onondaga, New York, were a successful farming family. In this era, it was common for people to take care of their elderly parents and grand parents.

Mary was Jeremiah's oldest daughter. At the time of this incident, she was also a widow. Mary was the widow of Judge Abner Chapman and had taken in family members who needed her help over the years. It is assumed that Mary was somewhat wealthy since her husband was a prominent Judge and a former New York Legislator.

According to the Marcellus Observer Newspaper in February of 1889, the village school had been closed down due to a small-pox scare. It is not certain if Mrs. Chapman decided to do her business outside of her home town of Onondaga due to the scare, or she wanted to have some time away or she just had other business to attend. Mrs. Chapman headed into Syracuse for the day and decided to leave Olive at home. News accounts of the incident claim that Olive was elderly but had been of strong mind for the past few weeks.

At about noon that day, Olive fell and by trying to catch herself, broke both wrists. It took her about four hours to get herself to the front door and to get the door open. Olive was able to signal someone who was passing by.

Her fractures were serious but Olive recovered from her ordeal. Olive Everingham died four years later and is buried with her husband at La-Fayette cemetery in Onondaga county, New York. Mary (Everingham) Chapman was born in 1827 and died in 1908. She is buried near her parents.

Grocer's wife
dies of blood poisoning

Millward C. Everingham was a business man and store operator from Fayetteville, New York. According to the 1892 state census of Manlius, NY, Millward was 26 years old and at that time he was a clerk at a local hardware. His wife Nettie was 30 years old and they had a one year old baby named Grace.

Millward or "*Mill*" as he was known, was entrepreneurial minded and later entered the grocery business with partner Albert Carr. The Everingham and Carr store was located on Mill street. That business dissolved and Millward eventually had his own store.

The store was located next to the Beard Hotel until the hotel burned in 1908. Mill's store was expanded and a gathering place, "hall" was added when Everingham remodeled the burned out hotel. Known as "*Everingham Hall*," it hosted business, town meetings and events for many years. Millward was successful in business and many of his advertisements (*like the one shown here*) can be found in old Onondaga county newspapers.

But before reaching success, Millward was struck with a family tragedy that could have pushed him to sink in despair. Wife Nettie was at home on Highbridge street, in Fayetteville. Some sort of reaction broke out on her body, particularly her face. Nettie picked at the inflamed skin and irritated the situation. Within days she had died of blood poisoning from her picking at the wounds.

According to her obituary, Mrs. Everingham died October 1st, 1902. She was 40 years old and had lived in Fayetteville all her life. She was survived by her husband Mill, and daughter Grace who was 11 at that time. Also surviving was a sister, Mrs. Bert Eastman.

Millward went on to marry Alice Duke two years later. His business success really started to happen after this second marriage. Daughter Grace is shown in the photo (*top right*) at about age 16, where she participated on the first Fayetteville High School girls basketball team in 1908. They called themselves the "wide-awakes." In 1925, Grace married John Kenney, who was employed at the Everingham family store. Grace lived until 1977.

Grace is the girl on the far right.

First girls basketball team, Fayetteville, 1908

39

The troubled daughters of Cyrus Evingham

Cyrus Evingham was born in 1847 in New York. He was married twice, had two daughters and lived to age 93, but the years were not always easy. Cyrus married Emma Roberts Wiley first. Emma was an attractive woman. Cyrus and Emma had two daughters that by all accounts were quite attractive girls. Being very attractive was certainly a blessing for the girls, but it turned out to be a curse for their parents. The girls caught the eyes of local boys who competed for their attention whenever Cyrus wasn't keeping them away. The girls were named Estelle Jennie, and Nellie Blanche. Unfortunately I have never found photos of them. The girls both brought trouble to the family by attempting to elope, stealing money and even attempted suicide!

The family first shows up in the 1875 State census of Amity, Allegany, New York. Cyrus was a 25 year old farmer and Emma was 21. Their first born daughter Estella J. was 2. Just 13 years later the trouble began as reported in this newspaper:

Buffalo Evening News, NY, October 6, 1888

Estella Evingham a young damsel of Belmont, ran away from home last week and came here to the arms of her lover, Rush Rockwood, late of Titusville. They were married before the girl's father could prevent, but he made it lively when he appeared. He had the boy arrested, but finally relented, paid the costs and went home, minus time, money and the girl, and a sadder and wiser man. The pair are as happy as clams

---

Estella was 15 or 16 when she ran away from home and married Rush Rockwood. She lived with her new husband until late 1892 when she deserted him due to domestic issues. In 1892 the census showed Cyrus and Emma Evingham living in Amity, N.Y. with 8 year old daughter Nellie. At the same time, while Mr. Rockwood was confined to his bed with a broken leg, Estella ran away.

Thursday March 16th, 1893, Estella visited her husband and daughter and told them good-bye, before attempting suicide. She attempted suicide by taking morphine. The local newspaper said that she came close to dying but two doctors worked over her all day to keep her alive. The newspaper reported; *"Mrs. Rockwood is only 20 years old and quite pretty. She is the daughter of Cyrus Evingham of Belmont."* Upon making a second attempt at suicide, Estella wrote a letter to her mother bidding her an affectionate farewell. The second attempt was also unsuccessful and Estelle went on to marry a second time to Edgar James Hyde in 1911.

The Evingham family troubles didn't end with Estelle. In 1899 *"Déjà vu"* set in as the family was again facing a daughter running off to elope;

Daily News, Batavia, NY, January 5, 1899

Will Crocker, a Belmont young man of shady reputation, eloped last week with 15 year old **Nellie Evingham**, also of that village. The girl took $200 in cash belonging to her father and the couple skipped to Shinglehouse, PA. They were finally located by Sheriff Hodnett at Olean, where they were already to fly to Buffalo to be married, having failed to find a minister that would do the job at the other places they visited. The girl still had $159 of the $200 in her possession, the rest having been spent for a gold watch and clothing for herself and her intended. They were brought back to Belmont and Crocker is now reflecting behind bars of the county jail.

By the 1900 census of Belmont village, Cyrus and Emma were still married and daughter Nellie was living with them but she was identified in the census as "Crocker Evingham". Either the paper had reported it wrong, or Nellie had since married Will Crocker but was living with her parents.

In 1913, Cyrus married his second wife Sarah who was 20 years younger than him. She had a son Gregory Wagoner, from a previous marriage who died in 1918 in WWI.

By 1921, Nellie (Evingham) Crocker, age 36, married a second time to Steve Romano, a Russian immigrant. That marriage was rocky. Nellie died in 1937. Cyrus died in 1940. Sarah died in 1959.

other Family News

INDIAN TROUBLES ON RESERVATION

Watertown, N.Y. Daily Times, October 1919

(*this newspaper is very hard to read, the actual news account is transcribed as accurately as possible*)

Syracuse, October 16, - Trouble between the Indians and the whites on the Onondaga Indian Reservation has developed and Saturday night a pitched battle between the two races. The ambush of a young Indian Monday by a quartet of white youths living near the reservation and an attack on the home of Mrs. Sylvia George an Oneida, with shotguns Monday night are the facts already charged up . Levi Hill, an Onondaga brave living on the Cortland state highway near the mouth edge of the reservation was the victim of the marauding whites Monday night. He was badly beaten after an ambush, his face and body severely bruised and several deep gashes in his head.

Dennison George, brother-in-law of Mrs. Sylvia George, was chased along the highway by a band an automobile. Felled to the ground by a short length of water pipe hurled at his legs from the car and then shot at with 10-gauge shotgun when he sought refuge in the house of his sister-in-law.

Robert Everingham, young son of Arthur Everingham, prominent South Onondaga farmer, is alleged by the Indians to be involved in the trouble. Mrs. Levi Hill, a prepossessing squaw, it is said, did the washing for the Everingham's and Robert, the son, called at the Hill cabin for the cleaned clothes. Mrs. Hill, it is said, took objection to his remarks and they approached the point where, for her own safety and comfort, she felt compelled to tell her husband, according to the charges.

A fracas in which Everingham and others and Indians were involved took place Saturday night at the store of Frederick Kane at Rockwell Springs, it is reported. After Levi Hill was attacked Monday night, Dennison George, a young brother of Leroy George, left his home to go down the road for some phonograph records.

He was chased by men in an automobile. He sought refuge in the home of his sister-in-law. He discharged a gun to scare his pursuers away, firing toward the fields. The men then opened fire at the dwelling windows being smashed and the buckets spilling over the bed in which two daughters, aged 12 and 14 were hiding. More than 60 buckshot holes were counted in the north side of the George house and 24 more penetrated the windows.

The affair brings to a head the question of the conflicting rights of the Indians and the whites on the reservation and the amenability of braves to the federal, state and county courts.

Another paper describes it this way:

White men and Indians have been fighting with fists, clubs and shotguns on the Onondaga Indian Reservation since Saturday night as the result of trouble which began when Robert Everingham insulted Mrs. Levi Hill. It is said that Hill tried to make Everingham apologize and a free-for-all ensued. Attacks and retaliations then occurred. The Sheriff's Department is investigating.

Greenville Daily News, Michigan, October 2008

14-year-old rescues his family in Sheridan, Michigan

SHERIDAN - *A Sheridan teenager saved his family from death by carbon monoxide poisoning Sunday morning.* That's the headline from the 2008 Greenville Daily News. Due to copyright, I will not print this modern story word for word from the paper, but that's okay... I should get the story straight, since I was there.

The story started one October morning when my 14 year old son Keric Everingham literally dragged some of his family out of the house, loaded them in the family van and raced to the local hospital.

As I recall, the adults awoke about 10 a.m. I noticed my youngest son, 7-year-old Kesen, lying on the floor shaking. I first wondered if he was cold, but I realized something was seriously wrong when I checked on Kesen and saw his eyes rolling back in his head. When you are overcome with carbon monoxide, your brain slows down so much you have a hard time thinking clearly. I knew something was wrong with him and I decided to take him to the hospital.

I noticed my daughter, Kaden, sleeping on some shoes near the back door and thought that was strange. I carried Kesen to the family van. When I came back in the house, my mind was hazy and I lost all strength. I dropped to my knees next to the kitchen table.

Keric then helped me to the car. My wife dragged Kaden outside but didn't have the strength to lift her. Keric, who remained free of symptoms throughout the entire episode, loaded us into the van. He had no previous knowledge of driving the family van but instinct took over. He got into the driver's seat and drove us to Sheridan Community Hospital which was luckily less than three miles away. At the time Keric said "*I didn't know what to think, I was just scared.*" As the van screeched to a stop outside the emergency doors, police officers and EMS workers who were standing outside helped us inside. The adults were hyperventilating and in a panic so we were hard to understand. At first they thought the carbon monoxide was from our van, but Keric was able to explain the situation.

My wife and I and the two youngest children were put on oxygen to counteract the carbon monoxide. After four hours of treatment we were all released from the hospital.

We believe that Keric was unaffected by the carbon monoxide because his door was shut tightly and he had a fan going in his room. He often slept with a window open, allowing fresh air. Sheridan Fire Chief Doug Lane followed us home to investigate the source of the carbon monoxide and found a broken chimney pipe. I replaced a rusted-through chimney pipe, and had the furnace checked the day after the incident. To this day, I begin tearing up each time I repeat the story. I expect it's due to the fact that I realize how close we all came to dying that day, and I felt terrible that any of my family had to experience it.

Keric was awarded a hero's proclamation from the Governor of Michigan and recognized at a special ceremony by the local VFW.

The Castilian Newspaper, Friday, May 12, 1911

FOUND - While boiling rags, Henry G. Everingham found a box containing several pieces of valuable jewelry which the owner can have by proving property and paying for this notice.

Henry G. Everingham doing the right thing!

This story is likely about Henry George Everingham of Castile, Wyoming county, New York. Henry was born May 19, 1874 in Castile and lived his life there. His grandfather came to America as a young boy from England. Henry was an iron moulder and farmer. He posted wanted ads in the local newspaper, stating that he paid cash for newspapers, books, magazines and rags. Was he an early recycler? It's likely that he found a way to make extra money with old paper and clothing trash. At this time, he had a young daughter and a wife to support.

There are no illuminating details about this incident but apparently Henry was boiling a bunch of old clothes for rags when he found a box of valuables. These could have been stolen or lost as far as Henry knew. He could have easily kept his new treasure and cashed-in from his find but he decided to do the right thing. He searched for the real owner of the missing jewels. He placed an advertisement in a local newspaper exactly as shown above. It was later discovered that the jewels were probably hidden in some old clothes that were thrown out.

A few weeks later this notice appeared the same local newspaper; "*The box of jewelry which Henry Everingham found in a sack of old rags a few weeks ago and advertised for the owner, proved to be the property of Mrs. Thos. E. Marsh who will probably use more care in the future where she places her valuables.*"

Henry outlived two wives and died in June of 1964 at age 90. He is buried in Castile, N.Y.

Red Bank Register, Red Bank, New Jersey
Wednesday, December 15, 1915

John Evernham Quits His Business and Goes Away.

The following story showed up in the Shrewsbury N.J. news section as automobile popularity began to change the carriage industry in the United States in 1915.

John Evernham has quit his carriage painting business and has gone to Brooklyn, New York, where he has got a job. Very few wagons are used hereabouts nowadays, the automobiles having crowded them out. Due to this fact, business in carriage painting declined and it was for this reason that Mr. Evernham quit.

American Artist Millard Everingham

Donald Millard Everingham was born in 1912 in Onondaga, New York. He was a commando in world war II and received the purple heart from being wounded in action. He was a writer and lived most of his adult life as an artist. "Millard" as he was known by the art world, went to Syracuse University and studied art. The photo below is his self-portrait entitled *"the awful truth."* He also studied art in Mexico and was the recipient of art scholarships. An article from the Eagle Bulletin Newspaper in 1945 says that he was the subject of a one-man art show in San Francisco.

His artwork can sometimes still be found today at reasonable prices.

Millard died February 6, 1951.

Other paintings by Donald Millard Everingham;

"Dead Man Alley-Winter" by Millard Donald Everingham, these are his typical water-color style paintings, 1940

"The Old Camp House", 1940 painting by Millard

Inventive Farmer Francis M. Everingham of Onondaga, New York

While this is certainly not a biography of Francis M. Everingham, it is a little information about this New York farmer who held several patents in the late 1800's. After over 20 years of genealogy and family research, I have found no proof of any connection to the farming Everingham family of Onondaga, New York and my family of Niagara, New York and Canada. The lack of proof does not discourage me from believing that this family is indeed related, but my inclinations really don't matter. This is just some information about a smart and successful farmer from mid-state New York.

It was about 2008 when I first did a search of patents and found the name F.M. Everingham.

I expected that this person was Francis, of Onondaga County. Francis had and uncle Jeremiah Everingham who's 3rd great grandson was Lt. Col Albert Everingham, a decorated military man that I was able to call a friend until his death in 2000. I didn't put much thought into proving this patent holder was Francis until I saw an auction posted in 2013 for an 1886 flyer printed by Kemp & Burpee Manufacturing Company of Syracuse, N.Y. I thought that maybe this old flyer would be an interesting conversation piece to have framed.

When I received the item (*shown here*) I was intrigued and had to learn more. I had previously read in various records about how prosperous and successful the Everingham family farmers were in Onondaga, New York. This invention of improvement gave a small glimpse of one reason why this family had such highly successful farms.

Record #316,886 at the U.S. patent office gives details about Francis M. Everingham's improved cultivator as well as diagrams of it's construction. Patent records are not terribly interesting themselves but they do give you an insight into the times.

This cultivator is certainly not the only invention that Francis came up with and many can be viewed by searching U.S. Patent records. He held patents for: An adjustable clothes Rack in 1867, A Harrow in 1887, A Road Scraper in 1887 which was an improvement on the earliest horse drawn road graders.

In the 1867 Patent, he was listed as Francis M. Everingham of Collingwood, New York. A later Patent in 1908 for a weeder attachment, further helps to prove who Francis was. It reads: *"Be it known that Francis M. Everingham, late citizen of the United States, and a resident of Onondaga, State of New York, deceased, did invent a new and useful Improvement in weeder attachments to cultivators, of which the follwing is a specification. This document is signed with the mark of (Maryette Everingham), Executirx of the estate of Francis M. Everingham, deceased."*

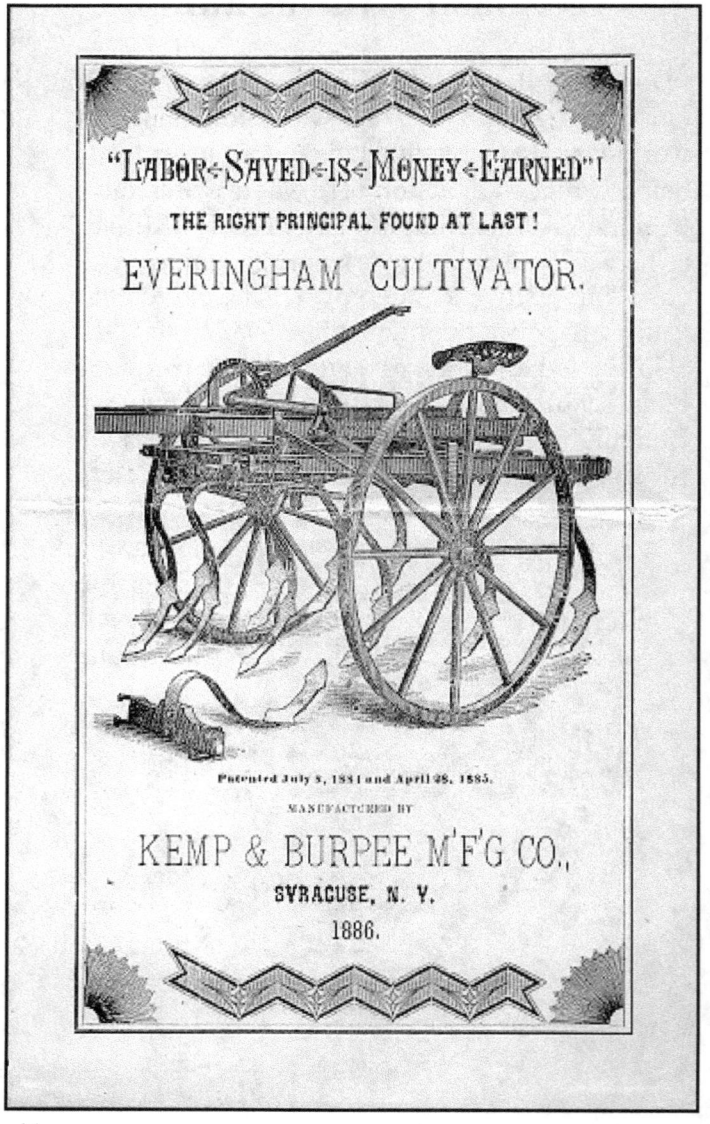

44

Syracuse Herald, August 21, 1917

Probe into the Death of Man Killed By Trolley

Motorman says Hyland Everingham was Lying on Car Track. Coroner Crane went to Fayetteville this morning to conduct an investigation into the Syracuse & Suburban trolley car accident in which Hyland Everingham met his death in that village last night. An inquest may be ordered. According to a statement by John Wright, motorman of the trolley, Everingham was lying on the tracks. Wright said he sounded the whistle and threw on the brakes. The car was then but a short distance away. Although Wright did all in his power he was unable to bring the trolley to a stop until after it had passed over Everingham's body. Mr. Everingham, who was 58 years old, had been a lifelong resident of Fayetteville. He leaves a sister, Mrs. Louis Washburn. and a brother, Peter Everingham. The body was removed to the undertaking rooms of C.R. Eaton.

The Pulaski Democrat, Wednesday, April 20, 1898

A civic minded woman and author in the family

Mrs. I. J. Rich has handed us a copy of a Kansas City Club paper which has an interesting sketch of the life of Laura Everingham Scammon, of that city. Mrs. Scammon is the daughter of Rev. J.S. Everingham who preached seven years in South Richland in the sixties. Mrs. Scammon was born in this state where she was educated and in 1876 she married Scammon, a Kansas City lawyer. In 1878 she helped organize a literary club from which has sprung over sixty clubs in Kansas City.

Mrs. Scammon is a prominent and active member of the Social Science Club which is doing much good in the west. She is a leader in other organizations, a writer of note and in many ways finds time to distribute help to her less gifted sisters.

DUNNVILLE GAZETTE, Ontario MAY 27, 1892

Killed on the Tracks

On Friday morning last, as Mr. Milkway, foreman on the section west of this village was going over his beat, he saw a hat on the track and working around found in a culvert nearby, the body of a man. Coroner Mac Callum, having been notified, had the body taken out of the water and it was identified as Hiram Everingham Jr. of Canboro, a track man. He was last seen by his friends at Canfield junction at 11 p.m. Thursday night, but another party is ready to declare that he saw him at Dunnville station after about 12 a.m.

A freight train went west shortly after that. It's supposed that he got on the train to ride to his father's house, about five miles from here, a little west of which place his body was found. He had evidently fallen between the cars, and he was horribly mutilated, his head having been crushed, and both legs broken. He was a widower, very industrious and leaves one child, it's mother having died about a year ago.

The Meade County News, Kansas, Feb 11, 1909

A Harvard Post for a Kansan

Richard Everingham Scammon of Lawrence, Kansas has been appointed instructor in histology and embryology in the medical school by the Harvard University corporation.

Of note - Laura Patience Everingham, subject of the top-most article above, was born 1844 in New York and died 1929 in Kansas. She was the daughter of John Stoughton Everingham and Jane M. Cowles, and granddaughter of Adoram Everingham & Patience Smith. Laura married James Scammon in 1875 and had two sons; Stanley Everingham Scammon, and Richard Everingham Scammon.

As the article above eludes to, Richard was a medical professor at Harvard and like his mother also authored books.

The Red Baron's victim #39 "Guy" Everingham

Most people have heard of the Red Baron. Manfred von Richthofen widely known as the *Red Baron* was born in 1892 and died 1918. He was the most deadly German fighter pilot *ace*, during the first world war.

According to the book "*The Red Knight of Germany - The Story of Baron Von Richthofen*" by Floyd Gibbons; Richthofen shot down a plane that was destroyed so badly that he was unable to figure out who the plane belonged to. He did pick up the number A2815. Richthofen flew a red Albatros DIII that day.

Second Lieutenants Keith I. Mackenzie and **George "Guy" Everingham,** (pilot & observer) were part of the sixteenth squadron and flew the A2815 on that day. Everingham had been married just seven weeks earlier.

The plane was said to be an old two-seater. The men were out on mission to make a mosaic photograph of the village of Farbus. They left the airdrome at 3:00 p.m. and less than two hours later observers in the village reported them shot down by a German plane. Eyewitness reports saw them break apart, fall and crash about a thousand yards west of Vimy.

Richthofen dispatched a German recovery party to the plane but a serial number was all they could obtain.

A week later, the English pushed forward and found the bodies of Mackenzie & Everingham near the Bois de Bonval and properly buried them there. The news was sent back to Everingham's young widow in northern Wales.

Richthofen recorded in a report; "*While scouting I surprised an artillery flyer. After a very few shots, the plane broke to pieces in the air and fell near Vimy. Plane was a B.E. two-seater, remnants distributed over more than one kilometer. April 8, 1917, 4:40 p.m.*"

After the incident, a nose-piece from the plane was recovered by Capt. John Haydon of the 42nd Battalion, Royal Hylanders of Canada. Nearly

Guy Everingham.

Robin Everingham.

100 years later, Mr. Haydon's grandson brought the piece out for public view. The canvas scrap with a "*blue stripe around a red nose,*" was estimated to have a value of £2,000 to £3,000.

According to the historical English book "*Visiting the Fallen: Arras,*" Second Lieutenant Guy Everingham, aged 22 and Second Lieutenant Keith Ingleby MacKenzie, 18, were both killed in action 8 April 1917.

Everingham was from the Colwyn Bay area and had originally enlisted with the Royal Welsh Fusiliers in October 1914, but after receiving his commission in February 1915 he became a signaling officer. In February 1917 while on leave, he got married, but returned to the front just two days later. Two years after Guy's death, his widow re-married.

Everingham's younger brother Robin, was killed serving in the Welsh military at Gallipoli on the 15th of December 1915.

Everingham Homestead on Everingham Road, Nedrow, NY

information from Hilda Everingham-Bittel, June 1999

Many family homes exist, but few stay within the family for so many years. The large family home at Route #1, Everingham Road in Nedrow, New York was built by Albert Everingham. The 196 acre dairy and grain farm and home remained in the family for at least four generations. Albert was born in the town of Fabius, July 24, 1840, and settled in New York with his father in 1850. Albert was the son of Jeremiah Everingham, a native of Cazenovia, who moved into the town of Pompey with his father, Jonathan, at the age of two years. Jonathan was a native of Connecticut, and one of the first settlers of the county.

The Everingham home was a grand six bedroom home with servant quarters. Hilda, great-granddaughter of Albert says that this home had solid cherry woodwork & staircase. After Albert lived there, his son, Arthur and his family lived there. The third and fourth generation of Everingham's to live in the home, was Arthur's son, Robert Everingham & his family. Robert's family included wife lyda and four children Lloyd, Helen, Hilda, and Al.

It was the largest home in Onondaga County, but until Robert and Lyda Everingham & their children (Albert's great-grandchildren) lived there, the home had no indoor bathroom facility. This seems strange for a home of such grandeur, but it was quite common in those days.

A family fight among in-laws

Kitty Sophia Everingham was born in New York in 1868. Sometime around 1885 she married Guy West. The assertion that Kitty and Guy's marriage was a bit rocky is based on the facts that she was at times living with her parents according to census data, as well as a few articles that were found telling about a nearly deadly family feud.

In 1889 A local paper ran a story about a family quarrel that was feared to be fatal. They reported that Guy West had previously married the daughter of Albert Everingham (*the same Albert from the previous story*) and the union was not made with the approval of the bride's parents. West was about 20 and Kitty was 16. Because of the lack of support for the couple, a secretive eloping happened. After married, the couple started a life on the West farm. After unknown marriage issues, Kitty took her child and went home to her parents.

Mr. West went to the home of his father-in-law to see his wife and child. The family stopped him and a quarrel ensued. At that point, Arthur Everingham, a brother-in-law became involved in the fight. West was violently pushed and Arthur threw a brick which struck West in the head. The brick fractured West's skull. A local doctor reported that he was unsure if the injury would be fatal. A week later, on July 24, 1889, the following story appeared in the Syracuse Weekly Express Newspaper;

"A family quarrel took place last week at A. Evringham's midway between Cardiff and South Onondaga. Some four years ago, Mr. Evringham's daughter Kittie, aged about sixteen, was married to Guy West, about the same age, and a son of Casey West of South Onondaga. The marriage was a run-away one, both families being opposed chiefly because of the ages of the couple. No serious trouble occurred and the couple began housekeeping on Mr. West's farm. They recently moved into part of the house occupied by Mr. West Sr. The two women did not agree well and lately Kittie came to her father's with her child. Guy came to have her return. This she declined to do unless he would provide room away from his father's house, Mrs. Evringham took part in the conversation and young West replied rather impolitely, calling her a liar and other names. Arthur Evringham interfered and

West dared him to the road. Stories as to which took the fist offensive move vary. West was pushed off the piazza and when he camp up again received a second push. Guy then came around by the steps when Arthur seized a brick and hit him on the head, which ended the struggle. Claims of fractured skull and broken jaw and perhaps fatal results are made, while other reports are that he is not seriously hurt."

Follow-up reports show that Mr. West did recover from his injuries. Both sides blamed the other for the couple not getting along. He reported that his marriage problems were due to her mother's interference. It appears that no legal actions were taken and young Arthur Everingham went on to raise his own family years later and lived until 1953. Very little is known about what happened to Kitty after this incident but census data show her two children living with her parents as late as 1910.

Police Officer Harry Evingham has his car stolen, 1941

Patrol Officer Harry Evingham was born in 1893 and died in 1972 in New York. Harry owned a gas station and small grocery business and was a patrol officer for the city of Wayland in Steuben County, New York. According to the local newspaper dated May 15th, 1941, Harry noticed his car missing and reported it.

That day the headline read; ***Thief takes off in Constable's car.*** The local paper also suggested that whatever the world is coming to is minor compared to what is going to happen if Harry Evingham gets a headlock on the fellow who drove off in his car a few days ago. Harry was unable to find his car shortly after reporting for work earlier that night. It didn't show up that evening so he reported the theft and a search began.

The following morning he mentioned it casually to a customer at his business. She had spotted the car, abandoned near Arkport, a small neighboring village. It appears that Harry was the victim of joy-riders. The car was found out of gas, but had not been harmed otherwise.

Civil War Union Army Captain organizes reunion

The following details come from a Crawford County, Illinois newspaper, circa 1923. The article discusses former Union Army Captain George Baxter Everingham and his family. It is reprinted just as it appeared in that paper;

Thursday last was a day made notable by a few of the old veterans of the civil war through the kindness of Comrade George B. Everingham and wife of this vicinity. Something over a year ago Mr. Everingham expressed to one of his Comrades of Robinson a desire to have some of the boys from Robinson and Palestine to come and spend the day with him. At about the time arrangements were making for such a visit, the home of Mr. and Mrs. Everingham was entirely consumed by fire. A new residence was completed at the same site, the invitation being renewed and a date set for last Thursday was accepted and the following comrades came to participate in the enjoyment of the occasion, their age in years following:

E. G. Rutherford 79, Joseph Lackey 80, M.J. Noe 76, Prevo Ralston 79, G. W. Harper 86, Robinson; J. W. Leaverton 85, E. O. Newland 78, F.M. Martin 78, A. A. Newland 83 M. H. Ambrose 76, Palestine; R. P. McGahey 78, Duncanville.

At the home the party was met by Reverend I. C. Tedford, son-in-law of Mr and Mrs. Everingham, who conducted them to the house, where they were received by Mr. and Mrs. Everingham, their daughter, Mrs. I.C. Tedford and Mrs. Edna Stephens.

The party having arrived at about 10:30 had near two hours of visiting and talking over old times, going back to a few years previous to the war in which they had borne a part and to incidents and circumstances connected therewith. The advancement in all the years following, furnished an interesting topic of converse and suggestions, as to what the future held in store for coming generations was a theme for some debate.

At about 12:00 noon, a call to dining room was made where the ladies had prepared a most elegant dinner. Seated around the board Rev. Ambross was called upon and returned thanks and the good dinner was disposed of with an appetite and relish, after which an adjournment was taken to the lawn.

Mr. Everingham, who is now 80 years old, enlisted in Feb.,1862, in a company being formed for a regiment which became the 62nd Illinois with James M. True of Mattoon, as a Colonel and S. M. Meeker, of the County, Major. The company was officered by Capt. Crooks, of Lamotte, Guy S. Alexander at first, and James McGrew as second lieutenants. Mr. Everingham who enlisted as a private was made 8th corporal, but sometime before the close of the war he had by promotions risen to the rank of captain, and in command of the company was discharged at the time of the close of the war.

He had saved some money during his service and was married about three years later to Miss Anna Musgrave of the vicinity. By good management and hard work he increased his possessions, and purchased the farm of which his present home is a part. The same good management has been able to help his children to a start in the world. Some forty-four years ago Mr. Everingham had erected a very nice, convenient and substantial dwelling of a story and half, adding outer buildings as they were needed, and this remained the happy home where the six children were reared, and married and settled in life. they are as follows; Mrs. W. A. Rains, Mrs. I. C. Tedford, Mrs. Ed S. Baker, Arthur O. Everingham, Mrs. W. A. Westner, mrs. R. L. Heber.

With this family of fourteen there are for the original parents 25 grandchildren and 10 great grandchildren, making a total of 49. The unusual thing in connection with the family is that they are all living, not a death having occured in all the fifty-five years. On the 15th of September of last year the home was burned, but Mr. and Mrs Everingham saved a picture of the old home where they had spent forty-three years of happy life.

As this foundation remained after the fire, as a matter of course, they wanted the new home built right there.

Lyle Everingham

College dropout at Michigan becomes head of a major U.S. corporation

In 2000, I corresponded with a 2nd cousin named Lyle Everingham. Lyle recalled memories of my grandparents and told me a little about his family. He never once mentioned that he was a very successful business-man. I guess it didn't seem important or relevant to what we discussed.

Lyle was born in Flint and raised in the rural countryside of northern Michigan, the son of Kenneth and Tena Everingham of Onaway. I knew of Lyle because his father was a first cousin of my grandfather. Many of the Everingham family lived around Onaway. Lyle served in World War II and upon mustering out of the military he signed up for college at the University of Michigan. He also began looking for work. His brother Bob worked at a local Kroger store so Lyle decided to go to work for the food chain. He started out as a bagger & stock-boy and over the years worked his way up within the Kroger company.

According to The Blade, a Toledo, Ohio newspaper, reporting on Lyle ten years before my conversation, he was extremely successful. After coming home from the army in 1946, Lyle enrolled in college at Michigan. After his first semester, he dropped out of college and continued work in the grocery business. Mr. Everingham rose through the ranks from bagging groceries, to cashier and becoming a manager. Eventually he became the chairman and chief executive officer of Kroger, which was the second largest grocery chain in the United States.

Mr. Everingham admitted that he had a fair amount of luck over the years, but attributed his success to his parents. Lyle's mother worked at Kroger and his father ran a small auto parts store. He claimed that his parents established values and old-fashioned work ethic. Lyle's brother Bob retired from Kroger as a vice president.

Lyle and his family lived in Toledo, Ohio for 11 years as he worked his way up within the Kroger company. From store manager, he became a district manager and then general manager. By 1963 he had become a vice president. Lyle was named president of Kroger in 1977 and the following year he became the corporation's CEO.

Under his leadership, Kroger eliminated many small stores and concentrated on the larger ones. They acquired a number of other chain stores and under his leadership operated 960 stores. They also introduced the concept of a combo store which offered a deli, flower shops, video rental, drug stores, banks and post offices, in one store. In 1988, Better Homes and Gardens magazine hailed the huge Kroger superstore in Cincinnati, Ohio as "*your dream grocery store.*"

Lyle is credited with keeping Kroger an independent company. In the late 1980's it was the target of various takeover attempts. In order to fend off hostile takeovers, Everingham engineered a massive restructuring that put Kroger deeply in debt and caused them to take a $119 million loss in 1988. The restructuring also forced the chain to sell some assets. By 1989 sales at Kroger grew 7.5 percent giving them a $18.8 billion cash flow . This helped them cut their debt by 413 million. Forbes magazine profiled Lyle's success in the May, 1989 issue. By the time Lyle stepped down as chairman and CEO of Kroger, investment professionals were recommending aggressive purchase of Kroger stocks.

He served as a trustee for the University of Cincinnati and along with his wife established and/or support several scholarships. He was featured in 2002 as one of the Chamber of Commerce's "*Great Living Cincinnatians.*"

After his retirement in 1991 Mr. Everingham became involved in many civic projects. As a result of his service in the area he lived in Ohio, he received honorary college degrees from Cincinnati University and the University of Toledo. As ironic as it may be, the man who dropped out of college at the University of Michigan and took a simple job at Kroger, achieved such success that he now holds two degrees.

Lyle didn't miss out on an education; he just obtained it with hands-on, hard work. He is the very picture of "*small-town boy makes it big!*"

A shipping advertisement poster during the Gold Rush, 1849

Gold Rush Fever in the Everingham family

The discovery of gold in California in 1848 sparked a rush to the area to mine for gold. As news spread, thousands of prospective gold miners traveled to San Francisco and the surrounding areas. These dreaming prospectors became known as 49ers, *the gold rush people of 1849.* The gold rush peaked in 1852 and it is estimated that over two billion dollars worth of precious metals were extracted by that time.

William Everingham *(shown here)* was born in 1823 in Ontario, Canada. His parents migrated to the United States and he married Elizabeth Sprouls in 1844 in Freeport, Illinois. By the time news of the possible fortunes found them, the couple had three children and a baby on the way. The family was established in Chickasaw County, Iowa. William age 27 and his  55 year old father set out to find their own strike and were actively mining by 1850. William's father Jacob was former militia-man during the War of 1812 and William later served during the American Civil War. They were likely a tough, hard-working duo. The 1850 Federal Census of California shows that William and his father were digging up a small amount of gold. No record has been found that shows us if they ever found their fortune. By 1851 Elizabeth penned a touching letter to her husband. She was patiently waiting for the return of her husband and simply wanted him to come home. She mentions their new baby "*Sarah*" in the letter.

1850 U.S. Census of Placerville, El Dorado, CA

(dwelling 1, family #10)... **William Everingham** 27, b.Upper Canada, value of realestate owned 600, occ: Miner,... Jacob Everingham 55, b.Upper Canada, value of realestate owned 800, occ: Miner, could not read or write. on both: (average product per day 2.25)

Elizabeth's letter to William:

> May the 21 1851
>
> Dear husband
>
> I now take my pen in hand to let you know that we are all well at present and hope these few lines may find you in good health too. I have got back to our little home once more and I expect to stay here until you come which I hope will not be longer than next winter or spring and I say to you I can do very well without gold as you are as dear to me without it as you are with it.
>
> I got home the first day of May and found things destroyed considerable it is useless for me to write a long letter till now whether you get this or not I have written you five letters since you left home. Which I do not expect you will get one of them. They was not mailed as they should have been.
>
> I will write something about your little boys and your little girls they are all well and hearty and Sarah can send her love. I would write much more if I was sure you would get it. So I will say no more, only; I remain your wife until death.
>
> *Eli. Everingham*
> *to her Dear and only love Wm Everingham*

One of Elizabeth's actual letters (shown below) recently sold to a collector at public auction for $325. It was simply addressed:
William Everingham, Sac City, Upper California.

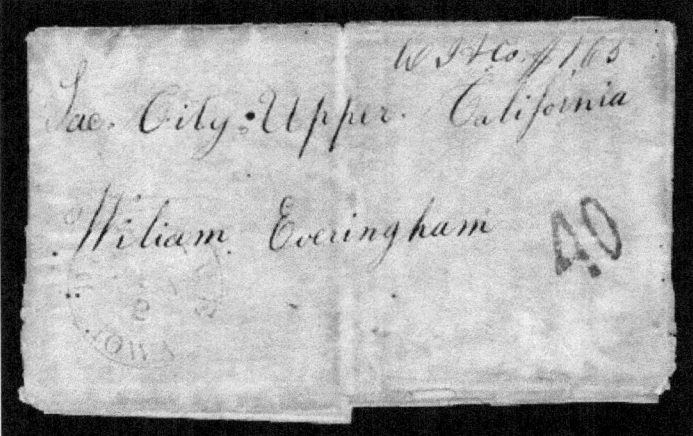

Family legend says; An old dog once traveled over 100 miles to find his family

My aunt Edith Everingham (*pictured here*) was born in Onaway, Michigan in 1933. She told me many family stories over the years. One of her childhood stories was passed on from her grandmother. When I was a young child, I remember her telling me about a family dog. She later re-told the family dog story in my adult years. Since this incident would have happened before Edith was born, she was relying on the word of her grandparents, having no actual proof.

According to aunt Edith, her grandparents moved from Turner, Michigan by wagon to Onaway, about 1907. Charles and Clara Everingham had a family dog at the time and left it with friends, because they were moving away. At some point the dog got loose and ran away from the friends home near Turner. After missing for many weeks, the dog showed up at the Everingham's new home over 100 miles away! The pet was said to have been in very rough shape & ragged. Grandma Everingham believed that the dog had been mistreated by someone, but after such a journey, many unimaginable things could have happened to him. Charles and Clara kept their old pet at the new homestead and took special care of him after that.

I have no way to prove this family legend and certainly stories can be exaggerated over time and this story is over 100 years old. I have heard similar stories about dogs traveling long distances. In this case it is tough to imagine because this dog had never made this trip and had no idea of the location where his family had moved.

Although the distance is very long, the dog needed only to follow the road north, which makes the story plausible. With a few jogs in the road and passing through the Huron National Forest and the Atlanta State Forest of northern Michigan, the trip would have been hard but not completely impossible. Finding food for several weeks and surviving predators, would have probably been his biggest challenges.

If this legend is true, the dog's trip would have made an interesting story that we will never know.

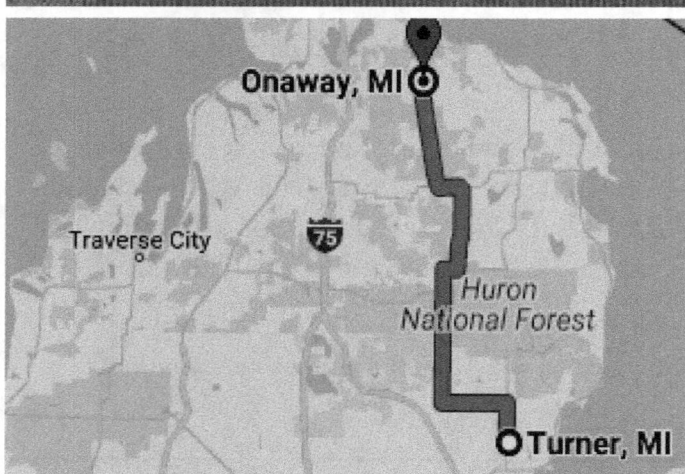

Traveling by car this is a 2 hour trip. Google suggests this is approximately 112 miles (if you stay on the roads).

52

Everingham brothers in the Newspaper business

Henry Everingham and Rebecca Currey were married in January of 1847 in New York and became the parents of at least a couple sons and a daughter. Henry's father was a wealthy cloth dealer in New York and Henry's grandfather was successful New York merchant Gilbert Everingham.

For unknown reasons, much of this family often spelled their name EVERINGHIM. This may have been the way they pronounced their name. The oldest son, of Henry & Rebecca was James Delaplaine Everinghim. James D. Everinghim was a news editor and publisher.

I first learned about the family of **James D. Everinghim** while searching for some information about a newspaper.

The *San Juan Herald* was published at the mining boomtown of Silverton, San Juan county, Colorado from 1881 to 1885 where it probably changed hands and name.

Between June 1881 and March of 1885 it was published by a company called "*Raymond & Everingham.*" That name caught my eye, so I decided to do some research. It was difficult to find more information about this company but I did find James and his family living in Silverton, Colorado according to the 1880 U.S. Census.

Further research uncovered New York news articles about James and his publishing which confirmed his career. He ran several newspapers, mostly in New York until his death in 1893.

These Everinghim boys were frail but smart young men. James started working as a clerk for a dry-goods store in Peekskill, in his youth. For several years he worked as a book-keeper for the coal industry. James decided to leave the coal business and went west to Colorado to start the *San Juan Herald* newspaper in 1880. He returned to New York two years later and purchased the *Peekskill Messenger*. Next he started the *Peekskill Critic* newspaper and likely owned, operated

B. C. EVERINGHIM.

or worked at several newspapers. He retired from the news business when he took a job with the Third Avenue Railroad Co. in New York. At the time of his death, he was secretary of the railroad employees association.

James had a brother named **Benjamin Currey Everinghim.** Benjamin married in April of 1875 at Norwalk Connecticut but like his brother, spent most of his life near Peekskill, New York.

Following in the footsteps of his brother James, Benjamin started working as a clerk. At age 23, he weighed only 90 pounds and felt that he was best suited for bookwork. His first serious job was that of an advertising solicitor. He remained in the newspaper business from that time forward.

B.C., as he was known, was involved in local politics and was a lifelong Republican. He was very active on his local school board and worked hard at several small political appointments. He once made the claim that he had personally met every Republican president and candidate for president, except Mr. Abe Lincoln.

Mr. Everinghim had written many articles about his favorite vacation activities, bass fishing and shooting. He was an outdoorsman and was part of the New York group of eight who held the world record for trap-shooting.

The Everinghim boys lived their lives writing and publishing in New York. Benjamin died of pneumonia in January of 1910 at age 59. His big brother James had died at age 47 of a stroke.

(see article about James' death on page 34)

Newspaper clipping about James from;
The Peekskill Democrat, Peekskill, New York, January, 1890

The Peekskill Critic made its first appearance. The publishers were James Everinghim of the late "Messenger" and Cassius M. Gardner, of the late "Idea."

EVERINGHAM MILLIONS
an EPIC scam

This article from the "Windsor and Richmond Gazette," Ontario, Canada, Oct 10, 1930

The story of Everingham family millions that were up-for-grabs, gained prominence in the late 1920's and early 1930's. A notice began to surface that geared it's mailings to people with the name Everingham.

Some of the mailings told about grand estates in England that were to be sold off, and how heirs were being sought to distribute the fortunes of the final sales of the huge Everingham estates. These scams were geared towards stories that made some sense in America, Canada and Australia. At the time there were people in those three places who were descendants of Everinghams from England and a possible link to riches were alluring.

According to an Newspaper in Sidney, Australia, in 1929, George Chaseling and Enoch Everingham of Hawkesbury were making a joint claim to the London Chancery Court for 11 million pounds. The money was said to be the inheritance of Matthew Everingham, who arrived in Australia in 1788. Shortly before he was drowned in 1817, he was going to England to claim his father's estate. Enoch Everingham was told about the fortune many years ago by a visiting sea captain.

According to the Sydney Morning Herald, Australia, November 29, 1930, (shown below) Australians were alerted that their oldest known ancestor "Matthew James Everingham" may have been a disinherited heir to millions of an Everingham family fortune. It appears that this story began focused on Australians, but the temptation of wealth didn't remain there.

THE EVERINGHAM MILLIONS?

AMERICAN AND CANADIAN BRANCHES

Mr. Leonard Everingham, of Ontario, Canada, has written to Sydney for information re the Everingham Millions, one of the Australian descendants having received a letter of inquiry. The Canadian Everingham is a descendant of Gilbert Everingham, a brother (one of three) to pioneer Matthew James Everingham (I.) (obit. 1817) aged 48 years.

Mr. Leonard Everingham hopes to reach Australia shortly, and is to take part in the plans and pursuit of the elusive millions in conjunction with the Grafton descendants of the first line of male descent from M. J. Everingham and his wife (nee Anne Chaseling) (II.). Mr. Edwin Lowe, of Mataranka, North Australia, and Messrs. Richard K. Everingham, and Abel Everingham, are the originators of the latest move to seek the fortune, which is said to exceed £11,000,000.

Many people were pulled into the idea of a possible gold-mine for our family, and wondered if maybe a great fortune awaited us Everinghams.

A story surfaced about an Everingham family in America that told of a man of high English society who had two "*or more*" sons. One son married the girl that his parents picked for him, as was common practice for the upper class in those days. The other brother, refused to be forced into marriage and was disinherited from the family's great prestige, power and money. The problem with this story is, that it has been used over many generations in other families and in countless fiction books totally unrelated to our family, for many years. The story continues with the one brother moving away to the American Colonies to start his new life.

Stories came from Australia relating to their Matthew Everingham and a possible connection to an American brother. Stories also made it to Canada as seen (above).

EVERINGHAM MILLIONS.

GLEN INNES, Friday.
A number of local citizens, who are interested in the Everingham millions, have been notified that a meeting will be held in the Newtown Town Hall on December 6 to raise funds to elect a representative to go to England and prosecute the claim.
It is claimed that several descendants of the Everingham family reside in the Glen Innes district.

February 21, 1931, the following headline appeared in Sydney Australia newspapers:

EVERINGHAM MILLIONS

False Pretences Charge.

DEFENDANT REMANDED.

This story said.... "What have been commonly referred to as the **Everingham Millions** were mentioned at the Central Police Court yesterday, When Alfred James Carlisle McGrath, printer, 54 was remanded on a charge of having on or about February 12, at Sydney and elsewhere, falsely pretended to the committee of the Everingham Estate and descendants of Matthew James Everingham that he had seen the Will of the late Sir John Everingham, Bart., of Yorkshire and Surrey and that the will contained the following, or like words;

John Everingham, Baronet of Surrey and Yorkshire in place of my will to recompense my dear son Matthew who left his Country with a slur on his name to go to a new Country with a stigmata on his name when a small effort on my part in going to court would have cleared him of this paltry crime, in that it made him leave his home and loved ones never to return. I might have saved him and by not doing would not have spent my closing years in sorrow and remorse. In having provided for my other sons, I leave my land and property, personal and otherwise, to my son Matthew James, his sons, and sons of sons and the trustees are the Duke of Norfolk and Lord Herries....

The Charge went on to allege that McGrath had falsely pretended that he had inspected the Public Records Office, Chancery Lane, London, the accounts and documents in connection with the estate of the late Sir John Everingham and that the estate at the time of the alleged pursuance of the records and documents was of the value of £23,750,000 in money and was being administered by the trustees, the Duke of Norfolk and Lord Herries, by means of which false pretences McGrath attempted to obtain moneys from the descendants of Matthew James Everingham, with intent to defraud.

McGrath was admitted to £100 bail.

The hearing was concluded at the Central Police Court, April 2, 1931. Of the 4 cases in which Alfred Carlisle McGrath, 54, was charged with false pretences in what is known as the "*Everingham Millions*" estates in England. Mr. Shepherd S.M. committed the defendant for trial.

Lawyers from the United States, Canada, Australia and England dug into the validity of the claims and a great deal of money was spent on legal fees. It was a nice boom to the law business, but no big fortunes were uncovered. Even after the trial in 1931, scams continued.

The following is a letter written in Ontario by a descendant of American Everinghams. This letter was written April 27, 1932:

> *"We are expecting news from or Lawyer in England by the 25th. There is a lawyer in Toronto who has written me, and asked me for all information of our branch. He also wrote me that I was an heir to the Everingham Millions, that is the way he put it, so you can imagine how anxious I am to locate all heirs. The estate will not be settled until all claims are in ... I will close, hoping to hear from you soon, excuse the way I have written this, but I have written so much to all our heirs that I am nearly done out."*
>
> Mrs. Alonzo Dell, Thorold, Ontario

In hindsight, it's easy to conclude that the lawyers involved had bad intentions and this was a scam from the start. In the moment, when you have high hopes of a huge payout, it's much easier to believe.

Today, we know that the Everinghams owned great estates, castles, and were the hereditary keepers of the very same *Sherwood Forest* of Robin Hood fame. The family also served several Kings, served in Parliament, held other public offices and had other important titles and riches in England. But by the 20th century, when the stories of inheritance emerged, all of this was splintered up among other families. Even the Australian claims to millions, which was probably the most likely story, turned out to be a far-fetched scam.

A family link to the Iroquois Nation

The earliest date that scholars can be sure of show the Iroquois nations were a unified group by the year **1142**, although the Iroquois people believe it was much earlier.

European settlers called them Iroquois Indians, but the people of the Iroquois nation call themselves **Haudenosaunee**. This term comes from the variations of Iroquois languages and roughly means "*house builders*" or "*people of the long house*." This is important because the Iroquois people built settlements with huge 2-story family houses, unlike other indigenous native people who built round houses or portable teepees.

As the map here shows, the Iroquois homeland covered northern New York and other lands in the 17th century along lake Ontario. Originally the five nations included; Seneca, Cayuga, Onondaga, Oneida and Mohawk. They were joined by the Tuscarora in the early 1700's. This group became known as the **Six Nations**.

As early as 1750, Benjamin Franklin wrote to James Parker referring to the Iroquois confederacy and noting that the colonists should form a similar union. It is believed by many that the Iroquois confederacy was the basis or at the very least, the inspiration of the United States Constitution. In Resolution 331 of 1988 the U.S. Congress officially recognized this.

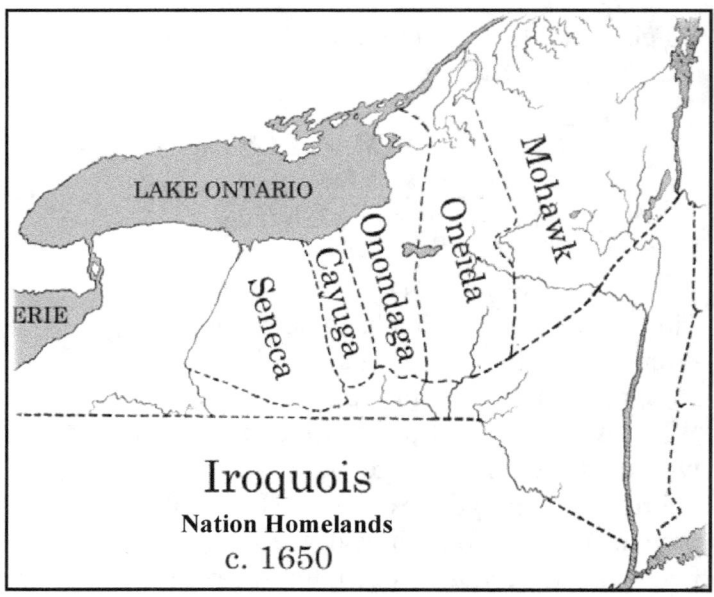

Iroquois
Nation Homelands
c. 1650

Much history is known about the Haudenosaunee and some of their great leaders but I will go into the history of connecting the Everingham family here.

Captain John Dockstader served as a loyalist for Britain during the American Revolution. He was known to have married at least four native women. He first married "Sarah" who was a possible sister of famed Iroquois Chief Joseph Brant. Because of this connection it was believed for years that the Everinghams of Michigan may have been related to Joseph Brant. That belief turned out to be unlikely since Captain Dockstader married second to a Seneca woman and third to a Cayuga woman. It was his fourth wife, sister of Chief Kaneahintwaghte of the **Onondagas**, where our connection exists.

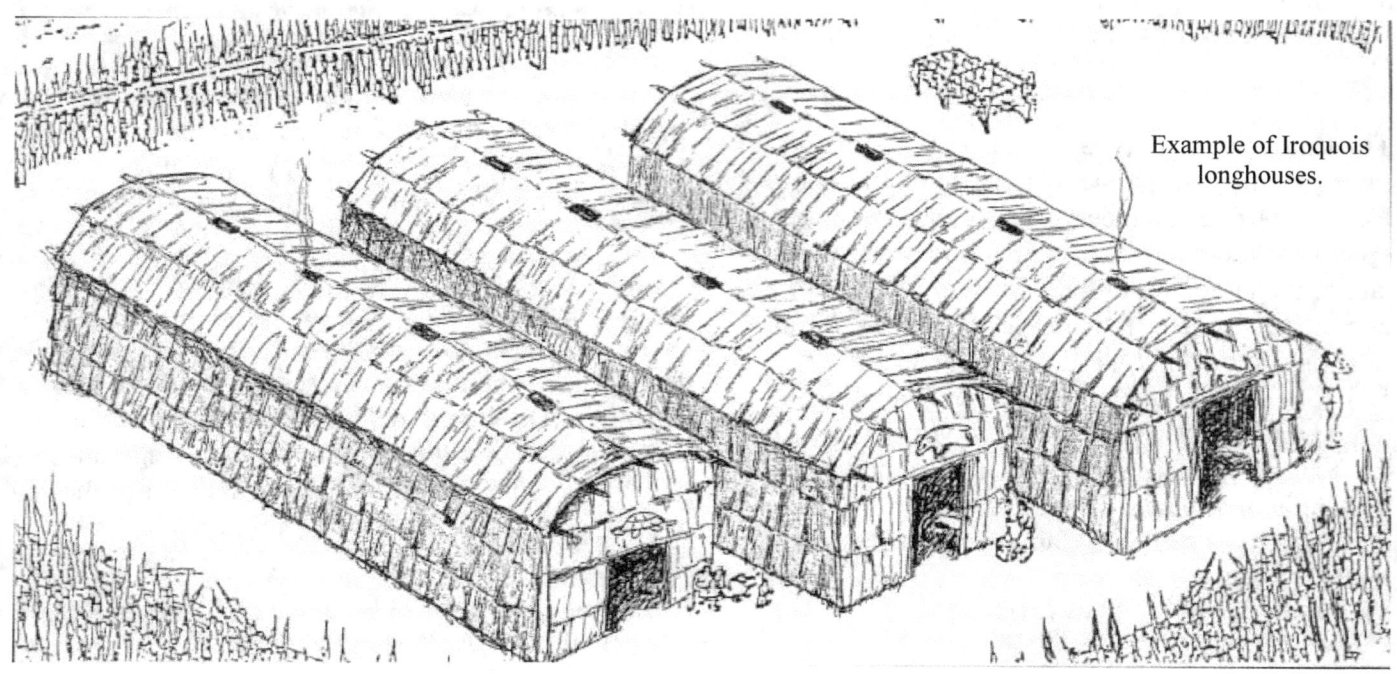

Example of Iroquois longhouses.

Captain Dockstader had at least seven children and had a daughter named Catherine who was born about 1788 from his last marriage.

Catherine Dockstader was a half-breed who married first to Chauncey Burnham. He died in 1807. She married a second time, to Lyman Burnham, Chauncey's brother. Catherine also had at least seven children including a daughter named Violet Burnham.

It was about 1845 when **Violet Burnham** marred in Ontario to **James Everingham**. Like Violet, James Everingham was also descended from a British Loyalist in the American Revolutionary War.

James was born about March of 1818 in Cambria, Niagara county, New York, which is just across the water from Canada, where his grandparents lived before he was born. Before James was born, his family was living in Niagara County, New York, but by 1830, his parents had moved near Haldimand county, Ontario, Canada. James was in his mid to late 20's when he married Violet Burnham and started his family in Haldi-

James Everingham (1818-1884)
Photo used courtesy of Donald Danskin, Saskatchewan

mand county, Ontario. It is completely unknown what Violet looked like. She was a white and Iroquois mix so some speculation about her appearance could be made. Unfortunately, there are no known photos of her. Violet was the connection of most Michigan-born Everinghams to Iroquois heritage. Each generation since James & Violet, one or more people are born into their descendant pool, with distinct features and dark skin, giving a hint of their Iroquois genetics.

James and Violet Everingham obviously had a very stable home, and many branches of the family seemed to count on them, in times of need, as evidence clearly shows. In the 1852 census of Dunn Township, Haldimand County, James' brother Hiram was living with them. At the same time, his oldest brother Adorams' daughter's Lucretia, and Selista were also living with James and Violet.

It seems that their extended family counted on them for a place to stay. Later data shows their granddaughter Cellestia Norris living with them.

On December 22, 1869, this strong family unit was broken up when Violet died in Onondaga township, Brant county, Ontario. Violet was between 36 & 41 years old when she died.

According to Ontario vital statistics certificate #3885/70, James & Violet's son Ira, spelled their name "*Evryingham*". He noted that Violet was only 36 years, 9 months old when she died of consumption.

Violet is noted in most genealogies as being born in 1828, however, when she died in1869, her son Ira estimated her date of birth of March, 1833, based on her age given. It is very evident from known records, that Ira was never very accurate with birth dates. If the widely accepted 1828 birth date is correct, then Violet was 41 years old when she died. Ira was the informant on a few of his family's death records which most likely indicates that he could read and write, as he noted in census records. Violet's death record also notes that she was born in Dunnville, Haldimand county, Ontario. Dunnville was originally a Cayuga Iroquois settlement. James Everingham died February 2, 1884.

Most of the children of James & Violet migrated to Michigan and raised families there.

BIBLIOGRAPHY of source material used in this book;

Court session minutes of Middletown, New Jersey, March 25, 1701
Monmouth Court of Common Pleas, Monmouth, New Jersey, March 21, 1770
N.Y. Journal or General Advertiser, No.1422, April 5, 1770
The Judges of the court of common pleas for Monmouth, New Jersey 1771
This Honorable Court: The United States District Court for the District of New Jersey, 1789-2000, by Mark Edward Lender, Rutgers University Press, 2006
Captain Chazal, Ship's log on the taking of the ship; Pelham, April 30, 1814
Disability paperwork of seaman; John Baker of the ship; Saucy Jack, 1816
Everingham Family History Archives (www.everingham.com/family) Est. 1999
New Jersey History, New Jersey Historical Society., 1877
U.S. Circuit Court transcript, Trenton, N.J. Oct 7, 1835
The American Neptune, Peabody Museum of Salem.
A History of Monmouth and Ocean Counties by Edwin Salter, published in 1890
Fare to Midlands, by Henry Charlton Beck, 1939
The Day Dixie Died; The battle of Atlanta by Gary Ecelbarger (c)2010
A Brief Record of the Life of William M. Wadley by Sarah Lois Wadley (1906).
Personal Diary of Sarah Lois Wadley 1859-1865. Historical Document property & copyright of University of N.Carolina
Naval History of Great Britan, England, printed in 1859
Congressional Resolution 331, (100th Congress, 2nd session, U.S. Senate) October, 1988
Forbes Magazine, *"featuring businessman Lyle Everingham"*, New Jersey, May 1989
The Red Baron Manfred Von Richthofen, by Pen and Sword, History book, 2009
The Red Knight of Germany - The Story of Baron Von Richthofen by Floyd Gibbons, 2014
Visiting the Fallen: Arras: North by Peter Hughes, 2015
Spink Shreves Auction Galleries, Dallas, TX., 2016

Thanks for stories and information from personal interviews with the following friends and family from 1990 to 2015, some of which have since passed away;   (special thanks for sharing your stories to help preserve our family history) Edith Prentler, Marvin Everingham, Tarry Everingham, Claudette Sabin, Leora Stierley, Bernadine & David Arnold, Hilda Bittel, Dale & Estella Black, Erlene Dudley, Albert Everingham, Ann J. Everingham, John Everingham, Kimball Everingham, Lyle Everingham, Bob Everingham, Percy & Mildred Everingham, W.Roger Harris, Grant & Marge Hayes, Tom Phillips, Debbie St.Louis, Inez Robinson. I have done my best to research and document every story in this book but mistakes are still possible. This book is intended to be an entertaining conversation-piece, not a genealogical reference book. (KE)

Chronological list of Newspapers *used in the research of this book. Many of the older articles are transcribed in this book, exactly as they were printed at the time of the events.*

The American Watchman Newspaper, Wilmington Delaware, August 6, 1812
The City Gazette and Commercial Daily Advertiser Christmas Eve of 1812.
The Argus Press, Albany, New York, November 1814
Charleston City Gazette, Charleston, South Carolina, July 21, 1814
The Rochester Republican, Rochester, New York, June, 1831
New York Courier & Enquirer, New York, NY 1834
The Long Island Farmer, Long Island, NY 1834
NY Spectator & Commercial Advertiser., NY. Oct. 2. 1835.
The New York Sun, Tuesday, January 19, 1847.
Eastern State Journal, White Plains, New York, 1851
The Daily Dispatch, Richmond, Virginia, May 23, 1853
The Western Reserve Chronicle, Trumbull County, Ohio, Wednesday, August 24, 1864
The New York Dramatic Mirror, NY, New York, 1879
The Highland Democrat, Peekskill, New York, July 2, 1881 & Sept. 9, 1882
Brooklyn N.Y. Union-Argus News, Thursday, Dec 8, 1881
The New York Times, Friday, December 9, 1881
The Red Bank Register, Red Bank, New Jersey,   December 13, 1881
The San Juan Herald, Silverton, San Juan, Colorado. (published 1881-1885)
St. Paul Daily Globe, St. Paul, Minnesota, November 29, 1882

Chronological list of Newspapers *(continued)*

The New York Sun, New York, NY, November 29, 1882
The Daily Graphic, N.Y., April 9, 1884. *"burning of the riverboat Rebecca Everingham"*
The Fredonia Censor, April 9, 1884
The Weekly Gleaner, DeRuyter, New York, April 10, 1884
The Eastern State Journal, White Plains, New York, April, 1887
American Newspaper Annual of Newspapers of the U.S. & Canada, N.W. Ayer & Sons, Page 364., Publ. 1888
The Cold Spring Recorder, Cold Springs, New York, June 30, 1888
The Daily Courier, New York Newspaper, Wednesday, July 17, 1889
Syracuse Weekly Express, Syracuse, New York, Thursday, July 24, 1889
Syracuse Weekly Express, Syracuse, New York, Thursday, July 25, 1889
The Daily Times of Troy, New York, December 5, 1889
The Peekskill Democrat, Peekskill, N.Y., January, 1890
Fayetteville N.Y. Weekly Recorder, Manlius Legal & Business Section, Thursday, July 16, 1891
The Auburn Bulletin, Auburn, N.Y., August 10, 1891
The Highland Democrat, Peekskill, N.Y., Saturday, Sept. 5, 1891
The Express, Syracuse, New York, February 18, 1892
Dunnville Gazette, Dunnville, Ontario, Canada, May 27, 1892
Syracuse New York Journal Daily, October 16, 1893
The Evening World News, New York, N.Y., Monday, November 27, 1893
The Syracuse Daily Journal, Syracuse, New York, Monday, August 13, 1894
North Platte Semi-Weekly Tribune, N. Platte, Nebraska, Tuesday, August 6, 1895
The Pulaski Democrat, Syracuse, New York, Wednesday, April 20, 1898
Sea Cliff News, New York, Saturday, July 2, 1898
The Argus Newspaper, Robinson, Illinois, October, 1899
Red Bank Register, Red Bank, New Jersey, May 30, 1900, Vol. XXII, #49
Watertown Daily Times, N.Y. Saturday, June 2, 1900
The Bolivar Breeze Newspaper, New York, Thursday, June 7, 1900
The New York Dramatic Mirror, NY, New York, August 4, 1900
The Evening Hearld, Syracuse, NY, October, 1902
Chicago Tribune, January 22nd, 1904.
The Evening Hearld, Syracuse, NY, January 11, 1904
The Wyoming County Times, New York, April 1904
Omaha Daily Bee, Omaha, Nebraska. Saturday, Sept. 23, 1904
The Silver Springs Signal, Wyoming, NY, 1905
The Castilian, Castile, Wyoming, N.Y., Friday, Oct. 4, 1907
The Meade County News, Meade County, Kansas, Feb 11, 1909
The New York Daily Tribune, New York, January 22, 1910
The Daily Sentinel, Thursday, April 13, 1911
The New York Sun, Historical Privateering article, February 9, 1913.
Red Bank Register, Red Bank, New Jersey, Wednesday, December 15, 1915
The Daily Colonist, Victoria, British Columbia, Canada, Tuesday, January 2, 1917
Syracuse Herald, Syracuse, New York, August 21, 1917
The Daily Times, Watertown, N.Y., October 1919
Paper name unknown, Everingham Civil War article, Crawford County, Illinois, circa 1923
The Evening Leader, Corning, New York, Monday, June 16, 1924
The Auburn Citizen, Auburn, N.Y., June 16, 1924
The Register News Pictorial, Sidney, Australia, Thursday, April 18, 1929
Windsor and Richmond Gazette, Ontario, Canada, Oct 10, 1930
Sydney Morning Herald, Australia, November 29, 1930
The Wayland Register, Wayland, Steuben County, New York, May 15, 1941
The Eagle-Bulletin, Manlius, Onondaga, New York 4/7/1944.
The Post-Standard, Newspaper, Onondaga, New York 12/24/1944.
The Eagle-Bulletin, Manlius, Onondaga, New York 7/30/1945.
The Blade Newspaper, Toledo, Ohio, Sunday, November 4, 1990
The Onaway Outlook, Onaway, Presque Isle County, Michigan, Friday, June 20, 2008
Greenville Daily News, Montcalm County, Michigan, October 2008
Star Tribune, Minneapolis, MN, February 16, 2010

www.ingramcontent.com/pod-product-compliance
Lightning Source LLC
Chambersburg PA
CBHW081418280526
45788CB00009B/3146